Ready Drafted
Legal Letters

READY DRAFTED
LEGAL LETTERS

An essential guide for
every business

JOHN A. NILSSON

PUBLISHED IN ASSOCIATION WITH
THE INSTITUTE OF DIRECTORS

DIRECTOR BOOKS

Published by Director Books,
Fitzwilliam Publishing Limited,
Simon & Schuster International Group,
Fitzwilliam House, 32 Trumpington Street,
Cambridge CB2 1QY, England

First published 1989

British Library Cataloguing in Publication Data

Nilsson, John A
Ready drafted legal letters
1. Legal business correspondence
I. Title
651.7'5

ISBN 1–870555–13–9

Designed by Geoff Green
Typeset by Wyvern Typesetting Ltd, Bristol
Printed and bound in Great Britain by
A. Wheaton & Co. Ltd, Exeter

CONTENTS

INDEX OF LETTERS

PREFACE

When a lawyer is asked to draft a letter for a business man he is given the facts and he then knows which particular legal problem he has to face. He has the law in his mind and a knowledge of the way in which, if all things go wrong, a case can be litigated and brought before a judge. With that knowledge he writes a letter which will fit the occasion.

That is the object of this book, to give some insight into the way a lawyer thinks when he is faced with a letter to write. The background law is given in very brief form, and in Chapter 16 the general outline of litigation is explained. A business is taken through many of the various problems that may face it from the first exchange of letters, when a business man purchases into the company, through the acquisition of property, the setting up of the conditions of sale and the making of contracts, to the problems of employment and dealing with agents and the various professional men (bankers, solicitors, accountants) that will be involved in the company's activities.

The business man who uses this book cannot expect to meet an experienced lawyer on level terms, but he will understand what the lawyer is saying and why he is saying it. He will be made aware of the pitfalls and traps that there are and he should be able to avoid falling into them.

John A. Nilsson

1

AN INTRODUCTION
TO LEGAL LETTER WRITING

Many, if not most, of the letters that a business man has to write are routine commercial letters or, maybe, social letters of greeting. The letters that give rise to difficulty are those that create some form of legal liability or are written with one eye on the possibility of trouble ahead.

Writing a letter that may possibly end up by being read in front of a judge requires careful thought and a good deal of expert knowledge. When a solicitor writes such a letter he will have in the front of his mind the legal consequences of what he is saying. He will use words and expressions that he knows will be familiar to the judge, and he may well have in his mind a case or an Act of Parliament from which he can make quotations, just as the layman might quote from Shakespeare or some other poet. A layman will, in all probability, not appreciate the law involved, and will certainly not have the advantage of knowing the way the judge is likely to respond. Often the non-lawyer will misunderstand the underlying point that the solicitor is trying to cover.

When people read a letter from a solicitor they frequently complain that it is too complicated, or that it uses language that they do not understand. The solicitor is not using some ancient form of English, nor is he trying to confuse. Just the opposite. He knows what points must be covered to meet the problem that is in front of him, and he knows how a judge will think. He knows the way a matter is litigated in the courts and can appreciate the effect that the words he is using will create. The solicitor realises that because he has become involved in a problem, there is a fair indication that the problem could end up before a judge, and he drafts the letter with that in mind. Laymen trying to copy a lawyer will use words and expressions that they have seen and think they understand. Too often they make a mistake and, through misusing legal terms, create an entirely wrong effect.

The purpose of this book is to try to help a business man when, without the help of a lawyer, he faces the problem of having to write a letter that is going to have some serious legal effect. (Every letter has some legal effect, but some are of more obvious concern than others.)

A word of warning must be given first. Where it is obvious that a lawsuit is very probable, consult your solicitor at once and do not attempt to be your own lawyer. (The old adage that 'the man who is his own lawyer has a fool for a client' is very true. He also has a fool for a lawyer; and that is worse.)

The first and overriding rule is not to use any expression unless you are 100 per cent sure that you understand its meaning. Be especially careful to avoid legalisms. Do not think that you can write anything you like simply by putting 'Without prejudice' on the top of your letter, or that the words 'Private and confidential' automatically mean what they say. They do not.

In Chapter 16 there is a brief description of the way a High Court case is prepared and conducted. It will be helpful to have some knowledge of the process. Once litigation starts you must expect that everything will come out into the open. Everything that is relevant to the dispute has to be disclosed, favourable to the case or not. Do not imagine that by destroying documents or by pretending they do not exist no one will ever find out what they contain. Over the very many years that lawyers have been working in English courts, they have learned how to ferret out the truth. In the witness box, being cross-examined by an expert, you will find that either you wish (Oh, how you will wish!) that you had not destroyed that piece of paper, or you will realise that someone somewhere knew what was in it and is making you look stupid, or, worse still, a liar.

The letters that have been written will be put under the microscope of the judge and of counsel on both sides. The meaning of the words that have been used will be argued over. If the expression 'etc.' is used, there will be arguments whether this, that, or the other is (or is not) intended to be in or out. In short, the letters that are 'legal' letters have to be very carefully thought through.

In the following chapters of this book, an attempt has been made to envisage all those times when a business man will come up against the need to write a letter that, ideally, should be referred to his solicitor. Some of the situations covered may seem very unlikely – it is, of course, when the unusual happens that help is most needed. That is why such out-of-the-way cases as a contract that becomes frustrated through government action have been included.

Obviously, it is impossible for a business man to refer to his solicitor every time he meets something outside his everyday experience. Even those businesses that have their own legal departments, or have a lawyer on the staff, cannot expect the lawyers to see everything. Apart from the fact that referring everything to the firm's solicitor would mean that he would be earning all the profits from the business, the delays that would be caused from that course would be quite unacceptable. The letters that are set out here are an attempt to suggest the way in which the solicitor would draft the letter.

In all of the cases covered, a possibility of litigation has to be envisaged. Any business man wants to avoid litigation and the objective must be either to avoid it entirely or to see that if the worst does happen you are in as good a position as possible to meet it. The drafts have been prepared with that objective in mind. The difficulty is that every letter must depend on its own facts and the draft letters must be adapted to suit the case in front of the writer.

To help in drafting the letter that the business man may wish to write, some knowledge of the underlying law is essential. To help with this a brief explanation of the legal principles that have to be borne in mind is given before each letter. The explanation is in general terms and does not attempt to explain every point of the law involved. It should, though, give enough information to enable the reader to appreciate the difficulties that have to be faced, and adapt the letter accordingly.

Use these letters with care. It is probably well known that solicitors use precedent books when they are drafting documents. They use these with discretion. The precedent helps in two ways: firstly, it is a sort of check list, reminding the draftsman of the points that have to be covered; secondly, it is a phrasebook suggesting an apt word or phrase that has been found useful in the past. It is not a tool to be used without thought. Some parts of the precedent fit what is required, some do not. Alter the precedent around, take some words from this draft and some from that, think about the legal points that are going to apply (if you have any doubt, do not write the letter without speaking first to your solicitor) and you end up with the document you need. That is the way to use the letters drafted here.

Each chapter contains letters which should fit the circumstances being considered. The reason why the letter is written in that particular way is explained but without too much technicality. Because of that, the explanation of the law involved is probably oversimplified. Do bear this in mind.

This is not a book that attempts to teach you how to write in stylish terms. If, though, your thoughts are expressed in a careless or confusing manner, it is more than likely that you will not achieve the results that you seek. A little time spent in preparing your thoughts and in composing your letter will be well rewarded. One of the great advantages that has come from the use of the wordprocessor instead of the typewriter is that the chore of retyping has been greatly reduced. Read your letter carefully before signing it and do not hesitate to redraft a sentence that you think is badly expressed.

Although this is a book about letters, a word must be said about telephone conversations. In Chapter 2 the point is made that in English law there are very few contracts that need to be in writing. You can commit yourself to a legal obligation just as effectively by a telephone call as you can in one of those beautiful legal documents all sewn up in green silk with heavy seals at the end. The trouble is that both parties to the telephone call may think that they agreed different things. Half of the conversation was taken up by greetings and commentary on the Test Match or the weather. When it comes to the real business of the call, two or three years later neither will have a very clear memory. Both will honestly believe that his is the true memory of what was said and will be convinced that the other is trying to cheat. A wise business man records his telephone calls with a confirming letter. As well as writing a letter, an even wiser business man keeps his telephone pad beside him when he phones and he notes down immediately what has been said. Lawyers always do this. They call them 'attendance notes'. Those notes do more than act as a memory, they are evidence that can be referred to if there is any dispute in court. So, be careful with your telephone calls and try to see that one way or another, what was said is recorded in writing. That way, if you have to prove that it is not your memory that was at fault, you have something to help you.

2

MAKING CONTRACTS

THE BASIC LAW

In English law there are very few contracts that have to be in writing. You can contract to buy a thoroughbred racehorse, or sell your motor car or build a dam, all without a word being written. Not only can you make a contract by word of mouth, but also (provided that you can prove what was agreed) you can ask the court to enforce the bargain. All that you need to do is show that there was an offer that was made with the intention to create a legal relationship, that that offer was accepted unconditionally, that there was some 'consideration' given for the offer ('consideration' is one of those technical words that need quite a lot of understanding – see Appendix 1) and that all the relevant provisions were agreed. In some cases (the sale of land is the most usual), there will need to be some written evidence of the contract. (Notice that the contract itself does not have to be in writing, only evidence of its terms, evidence which can come later.) In very few cases (the transfer of a company's shares, for example, or the giving of a guarantee are two of them) does the contract have to be in writing. But do not think that that means that you can get out of writing a letter. If the contract is left relying upon a conversation, not only is there the problem of remembering exactly what it was that was agreed, but, more than that, it is probable that only half of the really essential points were covered. What happens when something not talked about happens? When a letter is being written, more careful thought is given and there is less chance of a point being missed.

LETTERS WRITTEN 'SUBJECT TO CONTRACT'

As soon as you think that you are agreed, write and confirm what it is that you have agreed. If the negotiations are being conducted in writing, extreme care must be taken to see that you are not committed before you are ready. Most people who have bought a house will be familiar with the estate agent's particulars which are usually carefully headed with the words 'Subject to contract'. The agent is trying to be sure that no one can say that there was an oral agreement to buy the property and then show the agent's letter or particulars as the written evidence that is required. There is a trap here that you must watch out for. 'Subject to contract' most usually means that the document is inviting an offer to be made, and that until that offer is accepted no contract exists. It can happen, though, that the parties have reached a stage where they are fully agreed on their bargain but want the terms written out in a formal manner for other reasons. The words 'subject to contract' then mean, 'We have a contract on these terms but these terms will be replaced by a formal contract when our lawyers get round to it.' A contract exists. So even when writing 'subject to contract' be careful to see that the rest of your letter shows that you really mean that you have not yet reached the end of the negotiations.

Letter 2.1 is the sort of letter that would be written when negotiating with a prospective investor in the business. The writer of the letter wants to keep his options open for the time being. He does not want to be tied down yet but he does want to crystallise the current state of negotiations. He heads the letter 'Proposed investment' because he wants to make clear that, as yet, things are not finalised. In his opening paragraph he brings in the expression 'subject to contract' which, when read together with the heading and with the last but one paragraph, makes it clear that at the time the letter is written no contract exists. He does set out the important commercial points of the deal but he does not set out the detail of the agreement that his solicitor will certainly include; matters such as warranties that the accounts that have been produced are correct, that there are no undisclosed debts, taxation problems and similar worries.

Remember that this sort of contract does not have to be in writing. If you were to receive a telephone call after you had written this letter you could by mistake reach a full agreement. It is important to bear this in mind and be careful in what you say. The safest thing to do is to end the conversation with words such as, 'It seems as if we are there but let me sleep on it and come back to you.' In the letter the last but one paragraph says that the writer is going to get his solicitor to draft a contract. There is no need for a formal document with all its 'hereinbefores' and 'hereinafters'; the whole thing can quite simply be kept to an exchange of letters, although in a case such as this it would be unwise because of the necessity to cover various taxation and similar problems.

Of course, the parties may have reached the point where they have agreed the terms and want to record what they have agreed, but for the time being they do not want to be committed. They want to leave it until the solicitors have prepared a formal contract, or, maybe, they just want to say, 'OK, that's agreed but it won't come into effect until my birthday'

2.1

Negotiating a contract

Dear

Proposed investment in John Smith Ltd

Following the meeting that we had last Monday, I confirm the proposals that I made to you on the basis that they were 'subject to contract'.

1. John Smith Ltd at the moment has an issued share capital of £100, of which I hold ninety-nine shares and my wife holds one. The proposal is that I will increase the share capital to 1,000 shares and I will subscribe for an additional 400 (making the joint holding of my wife and myself 500) and you will subscribe for 500 so that we are exactly equal shareholders.
2. I will pass the necessary resolutions to appoint you an additional director of the company and I will arrange that my wife resigns her directorship.
3. We will then both appoint William Brown as a director. I will be chairman of the company without a casting vote.
4. We will ask our solicitors to amend the Articles of Association so as to provide that if either of us wishes to sell his shares he must first offer them to the other at a price to be settled by the auditors.
5. The existing solicitors and auditors will be retained and Mary Jones will continue to be the company secretary.

If you agree to this suggestion, I will instruct my solicitors to draw up a contract for your solicitors to approve.

I am very pleased to know that you may be joining me and I hope that our association will be a long and happy one.

Yours sincerely

(or some other event). In that case use the following as the opening paragraph to Letter 2.1:

'I think it would be helpful if I set out the points we agreed upon last Monday. Before I do so, though, I ought to say that we were both agreed that for the time being no enforceable legal relations between us have been created. This will be left until next September when I become sixty-five.'

SELLING LAND OR BUILDINGS

What if the negotiations are for the sale of property? That is one of the cases where written evidence of any contract is necessary. Writing letters on that subject should be carefully thought through. In English law you only sell or lease land. The fifty-first floor of a skyscraper building is land. A lake is land covered by water. This means that whenever you are selling an interest in a building, whether it is your lease you are selling or it is a freehold property or you are giving someone a licence to occupy part of your building, it is land law that you are concerned with. You are very unwise to try to tackle this without the help of a solicitor.

If you are going to attempt to write letters on the subject, be careful. The two points that are the most usual to cause problems are firstly the point that has already been explained: make sure that you are writing 'subject to contract'. The second point is to be sure that you are not saying something that could be considered a 'representation' inducing the contract. Here is another of those technical phrases beloved of the lawyer. It does not matter whether the statement was made innocently and the author really believed in the truth of his claims. If something is said that is not true and if that helped to persuade the buyer to buy, then it is possible that the buyer can have the whole sale set aside and possibly claim damages as well. This right (with some qualifications which are too technical to explain here) can be exercised by the buyer even after the deal has been completed and the property transferred. It applies to all contracts, not just sales of property, but it is in property sales that the problem is most often met.

Letter 2.2 is a letter which could be written on the sale of property. The letter is boldly headed with the words 'subject to contract' and these words are repeated in the text. The whole tone of the letter makes it

2.2

Negotiating to sell property

Dear

Re: Premises at Walsall

I confirm our discussions of today regarding our warehouse at Walsall.

Subject to contract, it was agreed that you would offer the sum of £25,000 for the residue of the lease which we hold on these premises. As I told you, the lease is for a term of twenty-one years from 25 December 1987 at a yearly rent of £12,000, which is payable quarterly on the usual quarter days. The rent is subject to review every five years. The tenant is responsible for all outgoings and for all repairs.

I am now instructing my solicitors to send to your solicitors a draft contract, and I hope that the sale will go smoothly. I assume that I will be hearing from the surveyor who will be inspecting the property for you.

We talked about many things and you asked various questions about the property. If there are any points that occur to you and that I can help on, please let me know. I must make it clear, though, that I am giving you this information in an endeavour to be helpful. Please tell me about anything that you are particularly relying on, so that we can see whether or not it should be included in the contract that our lawyers will be preparing. Anything not in the contract will not have any legal effect.

Yours, etc.

clear that there is no final agreement that has been reached. The last paragraph has been added to make it as clear as can be in a letter of this sort, that anything that has been said was not intended to have any force and is an attempt to exclude any claim that there has been a representation inducing the contract when it is eventually entered into. It is important that the solicitor who is to act in the sale is consulted at the earliest possible moment and that he has a copy of all letters that have been written to the prospective purchaser. Transactions related to the sale of property and any transactions that are contentious and likely to come before the court are all best left to the expert.

BUYING LAND

There is much talk about the English system of conveyancing and the time it takes to exchange contracts. There need not be any delay if the buyer has his money ready and the seller can move out without difficulty. In a business transaction conveyancing solicitors can (and very often do) exchange contracts and sometimes even complete the whole transaction inside twenty-four hours. It is perfectly possible to write a letter which is capable of becoming a binding legal contract. Letter 2.3 is such a letter. It has been said in previous paragraphs that there are some matters best left to a solicitor. More than most, this is one of them. Conveyancing, particularly commercial conveyancing, is not a matter for the amateur. However, if circumstances compel urgent and speedy action, or if for some other impelling reason it is desirable to proceed before instructing a solicitor, Letter 2.3 could be written. It is a straight offer of purchase and requires only the signature of the seller on the carbon copy to convert it into a full contract for sale.

In a letter of this nature the essential features are that the property must be described in such a manner that it can be properly identified. Ideally, a plan should be used, but for an established property with clear boundaries a general description by the use of its address would suffice. Beyond this, you must state the interest that is being purchased (in this case 'freehold', in other cases, leasehold, sub-leasehold or whatever it is), the purchase price and any other specific terms.

Because there could be so many other points that might come into question, it is usual to incorporate into the contract one of the well-known forms of conditions of sale. The National Conditions of Sale or the Law Society's Conditions of Sale are the ones usually used. Much is said about searches; in cases of urgency a personal search can usually be made. Because the point is so important it is worth repeating that although a form of letter is suggested it would be much wiser, if property is being purchased, to leave it to your solicitor.

2.3

Contractual letter of offer to buy property

Dear

Re: Freehold property at St John's Road, Aylesbury

Following our discussions, my solicitors have now reported to me on the personal searches that they have carried out on the above property.

I confirm the offer that I have made to you to purchase the property upon the following terms.

1. The property being sold is the freehold interest in Jimmy's Works, St John's Street, Aylesbury.
2. The purchase price is £500,000, of which sum I will pay a deposit of 10 per cent on your confirmation that this offer is accepted. The deposit will be paid to your solicitors, Messrs Chapman, Lee and Whitelock, as stakeholders.
3. Vacant possession will be given on completion.
4. The property is to be sold free from any restrictions or encumbrances that would prevent it being used for the purposes of my business as a brass candlestick maker.
5. You will deduce a good title to the property which will (if it is registered at HM Land Registry) be an absolute freehold title deduced in accordance with section 110 of the Land Registration Act 1925, or if it is unregistered will commence with a good root of title not less than fifteen years old.
6. Completion will take place on 30 September next.
7. The Law Society's Conditions of Sale (1984 revision) shall apply to the sale.

If this offer is accepted, will you please sign and return the carbon copy of this letter, and I will straightaway instruct my solicitors to proceed.

Yours sincerely

OPTIONS

It would be a very bold business man who would follow the course outlined above and actually commit himself to a purchase of land without having taken some advice. Time pressures, though, often mean that moving very quickly is essential. There is much talk in modern times of 'gazumping' and the risks that by not signing up at once an increase in price will be incurred by the buyer.

One solution is to take up an option on the land. Here you do have to expect to pay for the privilege and risk losing the option payment, but you do secure the position for the time being. Letter 2.4 is a letter creating an option. Immediately the option is secured it is essential that you register it. If it is a piece of land whose title has been registered at the Land Registry the registration is at the appropriate district Land Registry; if the title is not registered then two registrations are needed, one in the Land Charges Registry, the other in the district Land Registry. This is not something that should be done by the layman. Instruct your solicitor to do it for you.

Very often the reason for wanting time before actually committing yourself to the purchase, is the need to check that planning permission will be given for whatever is intended for the property. For example, a shop with living accommodation over it is ideal for use as a set of offices. Will you be allowed to change to this use? This is covered by the option proposal.

Of course, the terms of any deal such as this depends upon whatever can be negotiated. If you can negotiate that the option payment is returnable in given circumstances, good luck. If you are the one granting the option (you could rewrite the letter saying, 'I agreed to grant you an option on these terms . . .' and then set them out), you may be able to agree some formula under which the price goes up if the

2.4

Taking an option to purchase

Dear

Re: No. 28 The High Street

I confirm the agreement we reached today when you granted me an option, for which I paid you the sum of £1,000, to purchase the freehold of the above property.

The terms of the option were as follows.

1. For the sum of £1,000 (which I paid to you and you accepted) you granted me the option, exercisable within a period of six months from today's date, to purchase the freehold interest in the shop and living accommodation at 28 The High Street, Banbury.
2. The payment of £1,000 will not be returnable to me but, in the event that I exercise the option, credit will be given to me for that amount against the purchase price payable.
3. The purchase price payable on the exercise of the option will be the sum of £100,000.
4. I may exercise the option by giving you a notice in writing at any time before the expiry of six months from today's date or two weeks after the grant to me of a planning permission which will permit the use of the whole of the premises for offices, whichever is the first to happen.
5. I will immediately apply for planning permission and I will, at my own expense, use my best endeavours to obtain it. I will not, though, be obliged to make any appeal from a refusal. You will support my application by giving formal consent and support.
6. On my exercising the option, the Law Society's Conditions of Sale shall apply to the sale, you will sell to me as beneficial owner, you will deduce to me a good and marketable title free from encumbrances and, on completion of the sale, you will give vacant possession of the whole of the premises.

option is not exercised within so many months, or the price is calculated in some other fashion. All things can be negotiated.

7. Completion shall take place at your solicitor's office on or before the expiry of four weeks from the date on which I exercise the option.

Will you please sign and return to me one copy of this letter in acknowledgement that you agree these terms.

I am so pleased that we have been able to reach such a mutually advantageous agreement and hope that planning consent will be granted without difficulty and that I shall then be able to exercise the option.

Yours sincerely

SELLING GOODS OR SERVICES

A company is often called upon to give a quotation for the sale of its product or the service it supplies. Usually it wants to do this in a fashion that can be immediately accepted and create an order. Questions of 'subject to contract' do not arise. The problem that has to be thought about here is the question of making an offer that can be accepted. 'Acceptance' is yet another of those problem words for the British lawyer. How do you accept an offer? The terms on which the offer is made can say just how it is expected the acceptance will be demonstrated. Often one will find an offer (an offer of employment for example) ends with the words, 'Will you please sign and return the carbon copy of this letter in agreement of its terms', or words to that effect. An ordinary quote for goods or services will probably have printed conditions of sale on the back, and those conditions probably have a provision for acceptance. If they do not, or the quote is being made by an ordinary letter, something should be said about acceptance. Particularly something should be said about the length of time the offer remains open. Letter 2.5 is an appropriate letter to write.

2.5

Making an offer

Dear Sirs

As requested, the following is our quotation for the supply of 100 brass candlesticks.

1. Price. The price will be £2 per unit plus VAT at the appropriate rate, plus carriage.*
2. Delivery. Delivery will be within two months of the receipt by us of your order.
3. Payment. Payment is due thirty days from the date of despatch from our works.
4. Our standard conditions of sale,† a copy of which is enclosed, shall apply.
5. This offer remains open for one month from the date of this letter and any acceptance, which must be in writing, will only have effect when it is acknowledged by us.

Yours faithfully

---

* See 'Payment terms' on page 32 for an alternative to this condition.
† A form of 'conditions of sale' with an explanation of the various clauses that are used is set out in Appendix 2.

CONDITIONS OF SALE

It is modern business practice that a company quoting for an order will give its quotation on a sheet of paper which has written on the reverse (usually in letters that are too small to read or are printed in colours that are designed to discourage attention) 'Conditions of sale'. Companies placing orders do so on paper which in a very similar way have on the reverse 'Conditions of order'. Companies who receive an order frequently reply with a form of 'acknowledgement of order' and on the back are the 'conditions of sale'. What happens when the conditions of sale are different from the conditions of order?

A contract exists when the parties are agreed on all the terms, not before. If conditions of order are followed by an acknowledgement of order with different terms on the back, that is not an unqualified acceptance of the order, in law it is a counter offer. The lawyers have a great deal of enjoyment from what they laughingly call 'the battle of the forms'. Company A writes with an enquiry for the supply of goods with its 'conditions of order' printed on the back. Company B replies with a quotation with its 'conditions of sale' printed on the back. Company A replies with pro forma order, again with conditions of order printed on the back (so far neither company has accepted unconditionally the other's terms – the battle rages on!), and finally Company B responds with 'acknowledgement of order' and again has its own 'conditions of sale' neatly printed on the back. Have we or haven't we got a contract? If we have enough time and money to devote to this interesting question we can enjoy a week in the Queen's Bench Division of the High Court and perhaps find out the answer. Better by far to be careful and avoid the risk of dispute.

Obviously, it is going to be unproductive to spend time and money checking through every order and sale made by a busy company, but if the order is large or important this must be done.

2.6

Following an acknowledgement of order

Dear Sirs

Order No. 1234

Your form of acknowledgement of our above numbered order has been received. We have noticed that the printed conditions on the back of the form are at variance with our printed form of conditions of order. We do not accept your conditions and repeat our order in its original form. You may accept this order by proceeding with it without further written acknowledgement.

Yours faithfully

Letter 2.6 is a letter that could be written when an order is acknowledged with terms that differ from those that are desired. It is an attempt to win for the company placing the order the battle of the forms.

ACCEPTING AN OFFER

Each time that an offer is received or someone wants to conclude negotiations the problem arises; do I or do I not want this recorded in writing? If a written offer is made, and the terms are just right and you want to 'clinch the deal' there and then, the quickest way is to telephone the writer and say 'I agree'. But do not leave it there. Letter 2.7 is the letter to write.

2.7

Accepting an offer

Dear

Thank you for your letter. I confirm my telephone conversation with you when I told you that I accepted your terms and it was agreed that we would now proceed with all speed.

Yours sincerely

CORRECTING A QUOTATION

Of course, it is when you make a contract over the telephone that, as soon as you have put the phone down, you remember something that you should have said. Then when you ring back to correct your mistake you find that you cannot get through, or your caller has gone into a meeting and cannot be disturbed. It is all-important that you communicate as quickly as possible. Maybe, in law, you have made a contract, but no harm will come if you can make the correction before the other man has had a chance to act on your quote. Write Letter 2.8 and fax it through, if you can; if not, send it by first class mail.

2.8

Correcting a quotation

Dear

In our telephone conversation this afternoon, I forgot to mention that delivery cannot be made until after the works' annual break. This means that the earliest delivery we can offer is 1 September.

I did try to telephone you and tell you of this, but unfortunately you were not available. Please can you let me know whether you will wish to proceed on this basis.

I am sorry that this is the best delivery date I can offer and do hope that it will not inconvenience you.

Yours sincerely

PAYMENT TERMS

In every contract for sale, whether it is contained in some formal document or arises out of a telephone conversation, the terms of payment should always be discussed. If nothing at all is said, then payment is due immediately the goods are delivered. Usually business works on the basis that some form of credit is given; cash on delivery is the exception rather than the rule. Probably as usual as any term is 'payment at the end of the month following the month of delivery'. This has to be said, and in all the letters suggested in this work some provision is made. As well as specifying the time of payment, some encouragement to pay early (or, at least, not to delay) is often given. This can range from the penalty of interest on outstanding accounts to an incentive by way of reduction in price for prompt payment. It is a rule of law that payment of a smaller sum cannot discharge liability for a larger amount. There has to be 'consideration' for the amount that has been released. The usual way round the problem is to provide that the price is increased after a lapse of time. In Letter 2.5, for instance (see page 23), condition 1 could read as follows:

1 Price. The price will be £2 per unit plus VAT at the appropriate rate, if payment is made on the due date, or £2.25 per unit plus VAT at the appropriate rate, if payment is made after the due date. In both cases carriage is payable in addition.

GAINING TIME FOR THOUGHT

If, instead of wanting to accept the deal right away, you wanted to take a little more time for reflection, then clearly nothing must be written or said that could possibly be misconstrued as an unconditional acceptance. The clearest thing is to make a counter offer. (Remember the battle of the forms?) A letter along the lines of Letter 2.9 is called for.

Of course, it may be that you want to keep open your option to accept the offer exactly as it has been made, and do not worry whether the other side know that you want more time before you finally conclude the deal. In that case Letter 2.10 may be more appropriate.

2.9

Accepting subject to conditions

Dear

Thank you for your letter setting out your proposals. In general terms I could agree with your proposition but I would like you to consider whether instead of delivery being made on 1 April you could bring this forward to 15 March.

As to your payment terms, it is usual for us to agree to not less than sixty days from delivery rather than the terms you have suggested. Please let me know whether this can be agreed.

When I hear from you on these points I can let you know whether we are finally agreed and the order can be placed.

Yours sincerely

2.10

Deferred acceptance

Dear

Thank you for your letter setting out your proposals. In general terms I think we are agreed, but before I finally accept I would like to consider some of the implications that affect us here. I will come back to you with a firm reply in two or three days.

Yours sincerely

TIME LIMITS ON OFFERS

The point has already been made that any offer should contain some reference to the way in which it may be accepted, and some limit should be put on the length of time that the offer will remain open. As has been explained, an offer once made can be accepted at any time until it is withdrawn. Of course, there is a question of reasonableness – you could not expect to bind someone to an offer made twenty years ago, but decisions based upon what is or is not reasonable are always difficult to make. When making an offer always either withdraw it after a few days, or say for how long it will remain open. Letter 2.11 is an appropriate letter to write withdrawing an offer to which no time limit has been set.

If the time for acceptance has already passed, there is no need in law for anything to be done but none the less for safety's sake a letter should be written. (It is not only good sense from the legal point of view but it also makes good commercial sense to keep the matter in front of the other man's mind.) Letter 2.12 is the one to write.

In these draft letters the word 'offer' is continually used. Of course, it all depends on the normal terminology. A quotation is an offer, so may be an estimate, so is a bid or a proposal. Whichever word was used in the original letter, you can use it again. 'Offer' has the merit of covering all of these descriptions, and it emphasises to the other man that you have appreciated the legal effect of the correspondence.

It may be that having received an offer that is time-restricted, you want to ask for more time. Letter 2.13 is a suggestion. Always ask for written confirmation that your request is granted; without something that you can point to there is always the risk of misunderstanding or doubt. It is also very important that a request for time is made well before time has expired.

2.11

Withdrawing an offer not accepted in time

Dear

As you have not accepted the proposition contained in my letter of 23 February, I am sorry, but it is now withdrawn. I am still willing to do business with you, and would be ready to re-open negotiations with you on it if you are still interested.

Yours sincerely

2.12

Referring to lapse of an offer

Dear

I am sorry to see that you have not yet accepted the offer made in my letter of 1 April. As you will have seen from the terms of that letter the offer has now lapsed.

If you are still interested in discussing the matter, I would be pleased to hear from you to see whether it is possible for us to make a renewed offer.

Yours sincerely

2.13

Request for time

Dear

I am sorry that we have not been able to write to you on your offer of 1 April. We still have some problems to resolve before a decision can be made. Could you please agree that your offer can be extended by three weeks, within which time we hope to be able to respond to you.

Confirmation of your agreement will be very gratefully received.

Yours sincerely

COMFORT LETTERS

In the course of negotiations it frequently happens that one party wants to be reassured that someone who is not going to be a party to the contract will act in a particular way. The sort of thing that happens is that a major shareholder, or perhaps a large creditor, is asked to give some assurance that he will not step in and rock the boat. When a bank is asked to provide finance, it will often ask the controlling shareholders to give a letter confirming their support for the proposed transaction. The same situation often occurs when a subsidiary company is entering into a contract which it has gained because of the reputation of its parent company. These letters are usually referred to as 'comfort letters'.

When such a letter is being written great care must be taken. The question that is going to arise is whether the letter was intended to be more than a statement of present intentions which may or may not be carried out in the future (and which could possibly be changed if it was thought necessary), or whether it was intended to create some legal rights. Letter 2.14 is a typical form of comfort letter. The paragraph that states that 'no legal relations are being created' is the important paragraph. To make a binding contract there must be an intention to create a legal relationship. If there is no such intention, then there is no contract.

2.14

Comfort letter

Dear Sirs

We confirm that we are aware of the proposed contract between your company and our subsidiary Brass Candlesticks Ltd, under which your company will be making available a credit facility of £10,000,000 to Brass Candlesticks Ltd. We have read and approve of the terms of that contract as set out in your letter of 1 April. We confirm that it is our intention to retain our present financial interest in Brass Candlesticks Ltd, and that it will be our intention that the company should at all times be in a position to meet its obligations to you.

This letter is given to you at your request. In giving this letter we do so on the basis that there is no intention on our behalf to create any legal relations between us.

Yours faithfully

3

ENDING CONTRACTS

Contracts can be ended in a variety of ways and for many different reasons. Maybe the contract has been fully performed, maybe it was entered into for a set time, one or other may have so broken his agreement as to put an end to the relationship. It may be the case that the two parties simply made a mistake. They had not clearly understood what each had in mind. Above all else, if there is any risk that a dispute is going to follow, take advice at once.

MISTAKES

Where the contract itself has a mistake in it, that can be corrected. Where one party made a mistake unbeknown to the other, then he is unlucky. There is nothing to be done, he is caught by his mistake. Where both are mistaken, or one knows that the other is making a mistake and says nothing, hoping to take advantage, the contract can be ended. The most common cases arise where the letters exchanged contain some mistaken provisions.

They may be mistakes due to a simple error in the typing, they may be mistakes caused by bad phrasing of a sentence, or they may be mistakes where one party genuinely believed one thing whilst the other believed something else. If everyone is ready to agree that a mistake has been made and also agree what should have been said, a simple exchange of letters can make the necessary correction. For example, see Letter 3.1.

3.1

Recording a rectification of a mistake

Dear

Northern area agency

Following our recent conversation I confirm that there was an error in the correspondence appointing you our northern area agent. In paragraph (a) the initial period should have read 'three years from today's date' not 'three months'. I do apologise for this error and am pleased to correct it.

Could you please acknowledge this letter and confirm your agreement to this correction.

Yours sincerely

RECOVERING MONEY PAID BY MISTAKE

As a general rule, if you have paid money under a mistaken belief that you were legally obliged to do so, you cannot recover your money. If you paid it under a mistake as to some fact, then you can recover. The situation can arise where goods are purchased and paid for and then it is discovered that the goods did not belong to the seller (possibly because of a 'reservation of title' clause; more about this in Chapter 4, page 94). Letter 3.2 would be an appropriate letter to write. When writing a letter of this nature, in the first paragraphs set out, as clearly and simply as you can, the mistake that was made and refer to the amount paid. The last paragraph will then be a standard paragraph in all cases. It is prudent that immediately it is found that the mistake has occurred the other party should be told and the information repeated in writing.

3.2

Request for repayment

Dear Sirs

We refer to our recent telephone conversation when we informed you of the claim that we had received.

We purchased from you for the sum of £100, 100 brass candlesticks believing that they were your property, or that you were entitled to sell them to us. We have now discovered that, in fact, they were the property of Brass Candlesticks Ltd who have demanded that we either return the goods to that company or pay them the value.

We were very surprised to learn of this situation and, in the circumstances, we must ask that you return to us immediately the amount that we have paid to you, otherwise we will have no alternative but to instruct our lawyers to take the appropriate proceedings for recovery.

Yours faithfully

EFFECT OF MISTAKE ON A CONTRACT

If one party to a contract enters into a contract under some mistaken belief, he will be bound by its terms unless he can show that the mistake was brought about by something done or said by the other. If both parties were mistaken on the same point, then, so long as the mistake was a question of fact, not law, the contract can be set aside. Suppose that Company A agreed with Company B to buy a lorry which is being shipped to Company B from Scandinavia. Unknown to either of them just before they made their deal, the ship carrying the lorry had foundered in the middle of the North Sea and all the cargo, including the lorry, has been lost. The contract will be set aside and any money paid under it can be recovered. Letter 3.3 is the appropriate letter.

Obviously, no two sets of facts are likely to be the same. The first paragraph will set out the facts that were the mistake that both made. The other two paragraphs will then follow on.

3.3

Rescinding a contract entered into under a mistake of fact and requesting return of moneys paid

Dear Sirs

We were very sorry to hear from you that at the time of our agreement with you the SS *Scandinavian Carrier* had been lost at sea together with its cargo, which included the Volvo lorry we had agreed to purchase from you.

We fully accept that at the time that we agreed upon the terms of the deal, neither of us knew the true facts. Now that the facts are known, we regret that we have to say that in the circumstances we are treating the whole transaction as ended.

Will you please return to us the deposit we had made on account of the purchase price.

Yours faithfully

TERMINATING A CONTRACT BY NOTICE GIVEN UNDER THE TERMS OF THE CONTRACT

A contract that is to continue for a period of months or years will normally include a right for the parties concerned to end it by a notice. Any notice given must follow exactly the procedure laid down in the contract. If it is a formal document prepared by lawyers, do not try to give the notice without first checking with your lawyer and, preferably, letting him draft the notice. If, on the other hand, the contract was in an exchange of letters (say it was Letter 7.1), then the points to watch are that the notice is given at a proper time, that the notice is of the proper length, that it was served in the proper way, and that it is given for a proper reason. A mistake on any of these points will mean that the notice is bad; and that can mean that the other party now has some rights.

Letter 3.4 shows the points that may cause difficulty. You will see that, firstly, the part of the contract which gives the right to serve notice is referred to. Secondly, so far as concerns the expiry date of the contract, the writer is playing safe. He cannot be absolutely sure that the notice will be received in time to give the full three months that the contract requires so he gives a choice. Either the notice will take effect on the date mentioned in the notice or the date on which the letter was delivered. It will depend on which date is the last to happen. In other words, if the letter was posted on 14 December 1988, and was delivered by the postman on 30 December 1988, the notice would end the contract on 1 April 1989. On the other hand, if it was not delivered until 4 January 1989, the notice would end on 4 April 1989.

When letters of this sort are being written it is always best to ask that they be acknowledged in writing, and it is best that they are sent by recorded delivery post.

3.4
Giving notice to end a contract

Dear

In accordance with paragraph (a) of my letter of 1 April 1987 (the letter appointing you our northern area representative), I give you notice to determine your appointment on 1 April 1989, or three months after receipt by you of this letter, whichever shall be the later date.

Will you please write to me with an acknowledgement of receipt of this letter.

Yours sincerely

TERMINATING A CONTRACT BECAUSE OF BREACH

If one party breaks his contract the other has rights to claim damages. As well as asking for damages, it is possible to ask for an Order of the Court to make the defaulter carry out his obligations. If the breach is sufficiently serious (as the lawyers would say, a 'fundamental breach'), it is open to the injured party to treat the breach as a 'repudiation' and end the contract.

Very careful thought must be given to any response to a breach of contract. It may well be an advantage to keep the contract alive and seek either compensation or an order for 'specific performance' (another beloved legal term). It may be that it will be commercially attractive to take the opportunity offered and end the contract. Letter 3.5 is written to accept a repudiation and end the contract. Paragraph one should set out the breach that is being made. It is best that, before writing, some telephone conversations should have taken place (to try to find out what excuse is being made). The second paragraph is deliberately written in a 'lawyer-like' manner to give the other party the fear that lawyers have already been consulted. (They should have been consulted anyway.)

3.5

Accepting a breach of contract as repudiation

Dear Sirs

Notwithstanding the clear terms of your agreement with us and despite my repeated telephone calls to you, you have still not called off the third instalment of the goods.

I realise that you are having your own difficulties in achieving sales of the deliveries you have taken to date, but that is not a matter that affects our agreement with you to take 100 loads per month. This failure goes to the root of our agreement and can only be regarded as an intention by you to reject your contractual obligations.

I have considered the matter carefully and have decided that your conduct is such that my company can no longer continue with the association with you. I am advised that your breach of contract amounts to a repudiation by you of the contract and I am therefore seeking legal advice as to my company's remedies for breach of contract.

Yours faithfully

TERMINATING A CONTRACT WHICH HAS BECOME FRUSTRATED

When a lawyer speaks of 'frustration' he has something quite different in mind from the man in the street. When two people enter into a contract they take the risks that something may intervene to disrupt the whole deal. It does not follow from that that they can call the deal off because of something unforeseen happening. For example, a contract may be exchanged for the sale of a house and everything may have been going well until the week before completion. Then the house burned down. This does not let the purchaser out of his obligation to complete the purchase. He should have insured against the risk. If he did not, then it is his loss. Some things, though, are so unpredictable as to frustrate the bargain completely. The most usual are found in wartime, where state intervention cuts right across everyone's plans. It will be a rare occasion, but in case it occurs Letter 3.6 makes the point. As before, the first paragraph must explain just what it is that is considered to be the frustrating event, then paragraph two will follow.

3.6

Ending a contract which has been frustrated

Dear Sirs

Re: Software for Ruritania

As a consequence of the Order in Council made yesterday dealing with the supply of advanced technological matter to Ruritania we have been served with an Order made by the Minister of Technology forbidding the supply of any software under our contract with you.

In these circumstances, we can only regret that our whole contract is impossible of performance through no fault of either of us. We return herewith the deposit made by you and release you from any further liability under the agreement.

We are disappointed that our business should be frustrated in this way and only hope that when the present emergency has passed we shall be able to resume discussions to mutual advantage.

Yours faithfully

RECORDING THAT A CONTRACT HAS BEEN FULLY PERFORMED

In the majority of cases it is obvious when the contract has been fully completed. Sometimes, though, it may happen that in carrying out the job it becomes apparent that one party expects more than the other thinks he should give. For example, a computer programmer is asked to write a program to deal with a particular problem. As the program is being written, more and more aspects of the task become apparent. The time comes when the programmer says, 'Enough! This is something quite different from our original bargain. I've done all I agreed to do.' Clearly a dispute is possible. The programmer cannot write a letter that is going to put an end to the argument once and for all. What he can do (and what he should do) is put into writing what he considers to be the state of play. If he achieves nothing else he will start the argument off on his own terms. Again, as in the other draft letters, set out at the beginning of the letter the facts that are causing the problem. It is the very last sentence that contains the important point of the letter.

3.7

Claiming to have completed the contract

Dear

Under our agreement, as recorded in my letter of 1 April and your reply of 4 April, I agreed that we would write a program for your stock control. The specification of the program, as it was to perform, was included with my letter.

During the course of writing the program you asked on various occasions for alterations and modifications to be made to enable you to use the program in different ways. As a matter of good client relations, I made the necessary modifications and have not raised any additional charges.*

The program has now been written, it has been tested and runs according to specification. I have, therefore, fully performed my contract with you and enclose my account for the fee as stated in the contract. I shall be pleased to receive your cheque by return.

Yours sincerely

* If it is intended to charge for these additional matters, Letter 3.9 would be appropriate.

CLAIMING FOR WORK DONE OVER AND ABOVE THE CONTRACT

When two people agree to have work done, the extent of the task is usually outlined from the start. Either it is agreed that a fixed price will be charged or some form of charge based upon work done will be settled. Whilst the job is in hand it will often be found that other things have to be done that were not envisaged at the start. Care must be taken before doing anything. It does not follow that because you have done some work that benefited your customer, he has to pay for it. As one judge said, 'If one man cleans another's shoes, what can that other do but put them on?' In other words, you did not have to do it. If you did it without being asked, the customer is faced with no alternative but to accept that you have done it, but he does not have to pay for it. In these circumstances, before carrying out any additional work, make it clear that this is not covered by the original agreement and that an additional charge will be made. Write Letter 3.8.

Suppose, though, you did not write such a letter but the customer knew that you were doing extra work and said nothing, or, as seems to have happened in the case envisaged by Letter 3.7, the work was done at the expressed demand of the customer. Letter 3.7 may be needed, but with the altered last paragraph as in Letter 3.9.

3.8

Claiming for work done over and above the contract

Dear

Now that we have commenced to write the program specified in our letter of 1 April, it is becoming apparent that you are also in need of an extra program to cover a full database of stock and customer requirements.

We can incorporate this within the program we are at present writing, but it will mean additional charges.

You have the choice of leaving us to carry on with the present programming, and when that is finished having a new program written for the additional requirement, or letting us incorporate your additional requirements with the present work. Obviously, it is more economic to do the work now, which will save time and money for the future. Please, though, let us know what you want us to do. We would carry out the additional work for an extra £500.

Yours sincerely

3.9

Claiming payment for work done under contract and for extra work requested

Dear

Under our agreement, as recorded in my letter of 1 April and your reply of 4 April, I agreed that we would write a program for your stock control. The specification of the program, as it was to perform, was included with my letter.

During the course of writing the program you asked on various occasions for alterations and modifications to be made to enable you to use the program in different ways. I agreed to do this for you but as it was not part of the specification set out in our original agreement, additional charges have been incurred.

The additional work involved has been twelve hours of programmer's time. At the standard rate of £33 per hour (which is the normal and accepted rate for this type of work), this involves a fee of £396.

The program has now been written with the modifications you requested. It has been tested and runs according to specification. I have, therefore, fully performed my contract with you and enclose my account for the fee as stated in the contract, plus an additional charge of £396 for the additional work.

I shall be pleased to receive your cheque by return.

Yours sincerely

RECORDING THE END OF A CONTRACT THROUGH PASSAGE OF TIME

When an agreement is entered into for a fixed period and when that time comes to an end it is advisable to write and say so. If you do not do this a problem is going to arise. Suppose that you carry on doing business together, are you extending the contract (so that all the old terms still apply) or are you starting out on a new deal with the old arrangement to be forgotten? Write and make clear what is happening so that possible misunderstandings can be avoided.

3.10

Confirming contract ended

Dear

It is sad to realise that the three years during which we agreed to co-operate in the sale of brass candlesticks will end on 1 April.

I hope that we can continue to work together in the future as in the past.

Do you want to agree a new contract or would you prefer that from now on we treat each opportunity as a separate matter to be looked at on its own facts? I am quite open minded and am happy to see you at any time to work out the way we will proceed in the future.

Best wishes to you and I look forward to our meeting together soon.

Yours sincerely

4

SALE OF GOODS

GOODS ON APPROVAL

When goods are despatched before they are paid for, the supplier is taking a calculated risk; will the bill be paid? Of course, if the customer is well known and trusted one does not hesitate. In many cases, though, business means that risks must be taken to make a sale. The risk being faced is not just the risk that there may be difficulty in collecting the purchase price, there is also the risk that the goods may be taken by another creditor or be seized by a receiver or a liquidator. The important point to be covered is what the lawyers would describe as the 'property' in the goods. 'Property' could loosely be described as the true ownership of the goods.

Modern conditions of sale usually have a condition which says words to the effect that 'the property in the goods shall remain in the seller until all payments due in respect of them have been made'. (That is what is called a retention of title clause; it is explained in more detail on page 94.) The same problem has to be faced when goods are sent on approval or on sale or return. Any goods sent like that must be covered by a letter which makes it clear that until payment is made the ownership of the goods remain with the person selling them. Letter 4.1 is an example. It is probable that the goods themselves will be despatched by carrier, and that the letter will not be with them. The containers should be clearly marked with the name and address of the seller and have the words 'Despatched under reservation of title' stamped on them.

Letter 4.1 is drafted on the assumption that the goods in question were requested by the possible buyer and that the buyer is a business, not a consumer. If they were not specifically requested, Letter 4.2 will be the one to look at. Consumer sales are dealt with on page 74.

4.1

Goods sent on approval

Dear Sirs

In response to your recent request for an opportunity to inspect our range of brass candlesticks, we have sent by separate delivery a sample of each model for your approval.

You may retain them for a period of ten days after which they should be returned, for which purpose a redelivery label is enclosed. Any goods not returned within this period will be deemed to have been accepted by you and the full purchase price, as set out on our enclosed price list, will be payable.

Our terms of business, including payment terms, are set out on the reverse of this letter. We particularly draw your attention to condition 3 of our terms, which provides that this delivery is despatched on the basis that the ownership of the goods will not pass to you until payment has been made in full.

We also draw your attention to the fact that so long as you retain the goods you will be responsible for any loss or damage to them.

We hope that you will be pleased with our range and that we shall have the pleasure of developing a business relationship with you.

Yours faithfully

GOODS SENT ON APPROVAL WITHOUT PRIOR REQUEST

If there are dangers in despatching goods on request and without prior payment, there are even greater dangers in sending out unsolicited goods. Most lawyers would say that this should only be done if you are willing to write off the value of the goods at the outset.

Firstly, there is the risk that the goods will be taken and not paid for. Secondly, there is the risk that the goods will be lost or damaged and no compensation can be recovered. Lastly, there is the problem of recovery of the goods if they are rejected.

There is no obligation on the receiver of the goods to acknowledge them, to take any particular care of them or to return them, and if they are not reclaimed by the seller within six months they are considered to be an unconditional gift. The best that can be done is to try to get some protection from possible claims by others. Letter 4.2 is about the best that can be done.

Notice the sentence about the risk of damage. The point of this sentence is to try to get some protection in case the goods are not properly protected. The law is not clear on the point, but whilst there is no specific duty on the receiver of the goods to look after them, he could be liable if they are damaged because he deliberately mistreated them or was reckless in the way they were cared for. The object of the sentence is to draw attention to the way in which the goods could be damaged and thereby give some argument that they have been deliberately or recklessly mistreated.

4.2

Unsolicited goods

Dear Customer

As an introduction to our range of speciality glassware we are sending to you a sample of some of our latest designs, together with a leaflet giving details of the prices and normal business terms which we offer.

All the glasses are made of the finest glass. They are fragile, can easily be damaged, and because of the quality should not be allowed to be exposed to extremes of temperature.

We will telephone you within the next few days, after you have had an opportunity to inspect the goods, to discuss with you any points you may wish to raise. You are, of course, under no obligation to purchase any of the goods, which since they will belong to us until you purchase them, will be entirely at our risk whilst they are on your premises.

We look forward to speaking to you and hope that we will have the pleasure of doing business with you.

Yours faithfully

CONSUMER SALES

This is probably the age of the consumer. (This is another term which lawyers find difficult – see Appendix 1.) Whilst sales to businesses can impose conditions, sales to consumers are hedged about with restrictions. The consumer is given warranties which cannot be excluded. In an ordinary business sale it is possible sometimes to limit claims by writing what lawyers call exclusion clauses. This is too big a subject for this work. In consumer sales, that is to say a sale to someone who is not buying for the purpose of his business, exclusion clauses are very difficult. If any form of credit is offered even more restrictions are imposed upon the seller. Because of the dangers involved in sending goods to a 'consumer' who has not ordered them no suggested covering letter is included. In other cases Letter 4.3 may be of help.

4.3

Accompanying a consumer sale of goods

Dear Sir/Madam

We are very pleased to have received your letter, and are sending by separate despatch the goods requested. All our goods are sold on our standard trading terms (a copy of which is enclosed) which include our guarantee of reliability. A certificate confirming your guarantee is enclosed. Our invoice is also enclosed for payment by you as soon as you safely receive the goods and are satisfied with them.

Yours faithfully

One of the worst consequences of a claim that there is something wrong with the goods is the adverse publicity that results. There is, in practical terms, little that can be done to stop the bad publicity that comes when press, radio or television investigation is encountered. It can be possible, though, to limit the damage caused by a genuine dispute which would otherwise have to be the subject of litigation.

A 'lawyer-like' letter might be too offputting, but the effect can be achieved by including the required point in a certificate of guarantee. A suggested form (which can, in its first paragraph, be adapted to cover whatever is the normal guarantee given) is set out opposite. Paragraph 2 of the form of guarantee is an agreement to arbitrate any dispute instead of going to litigation. An arbitration can be conducted in private and without the glare of the publicity that would follow a case in court. The letter presupposes that there have been no formal 'conditions of sale' used. Paragraph 1 is designed to make this an 'offer' (remember the battle of the forms described in Chapter 2, page 24). The plot only works if the customer signs and returns the guarantee, because an agreement to arbitrate has to be a mutual agreement. If he does not accept the guarantee, then he has not accepted the agreement to arbitrate.

Certificate of guarantee

In addition to all the rights given by statute, we hereby guarantee all goods supplied for a period of twelve months from the date of purchase. Except for any defects or faults caused through misuse we will, at our discretion, either carry out a complete repair free of all charges or replace the defective product. Your rights under the Sale of Goods Act 1979, and any other statutory rights, are not affected.

Any claim as to the goods shall be made under the terms of this guarantee and in the event that there shall be any dispute which arises in respect of or incidental to the goods it shall be referred to the arbitration of a single arbitrator to be appointed (in case of dispute) by the President of the London Court of Arbitration. The rules of the London Court of Arbitration shall apply to the arbitration. The tear-off portion of this guarantee must be returned to us to accept its terms.

REJECTING DELIVERY

When goods are sold by description or by sample, if they do not correspond with the description or are not up to sample, they can be rejected. In the same way, where goods are delivered in a damaged state, they can be rejected. The right to reject is lost if delivery is accepted. There may be a right to claim damages but the buyer, having accepted them, must keep them. The buyer must be given the opportunity to inspect the goods to satisfy himself that they do conform to the order, and if he is not satisfied he must reject them. Letter 4.4 is a letter of rejection because the goods did not conform to sample (or description, or were damaged).

The same principle applies to late delivery. If the order required delivery to be made by a specific time, then late delivery gives a right to reject. Of course, it also gives a right to accept and claim damages. The question of claims for damages is dealt with in the next chapter. Letter 4.5 is a letter of rejection where delivery was attempted out of time. In both letters it has been assumed that the carrier has taken the goods away. Of course, some carriers are not so co-operative, and having offloaded the goods refuse point blank to have anything more to do with them. Letter 4.6 deals with this point.

A word of warning: the practice of taking delivery, whilst marking the delivery note 'Received unexamined', has doubtful value when considered against the seller of the goods. The buyer has to be given a reasonable chance to examine the goods before deciding whether or not to accept them, and he is given a reasonable time to carry out his examination and notify rejection. If there is no attempt made to examine the goods when delivery is made, the right to reject may have been lost. Of course, there is a different point as between the carrier and the acceptor of delivery. Many contracts of carriage would keep open

4.4

Rejecting goods

Dear Sirs

Our order no.

Your carrier today attempted to deliver goods said to be in fulfilment of our above-numbered order.

On examination we found that the goods offered did not correspond with the sample we had received [with the description given/were damaged] and we refused to accept them. The carrier was instructed to return them to you.

Yours faithfully

rights to claim that damage had been caused in transit even though delivery had been taken. That, though, is not the point being considered here.

4.5

Rejecting goods because of late delivery

Dear Sirs

Our order no.

Your carrier today attempted to deliver goods pursuant to our above-quoted order.

It was a fundamental term of our order that the goods would be delivered by the 1st of this month. In view of your failure to comply with this term, we refuse to accept the goods and have instructed your carrier to return them to you.

Your failure has caused us loss and a further letter will be sent to you on this subject.

Yours faithfully

4.6

Where carrier left goods

Dear Sirs

Our order no.

[Paragraph 1 as in previous letter.]

The carrier was instructed to return the goods to you. [Or, if it is the case, 'The carrier left before we could give him instructions to return the goods to you.']

We have given no permission, expressly or by implication, permitting the goods to be left on our premises. We require you to remove them immediately and accept no liability for them or for any damage that they may suffer whilst they are on our premises.

Yours faithfully

ACCEPTING DELIVERY

As indicated above, instead of rejecting the goods the buyer can accept them and claim damages. The difficulty with that course is arriving at the amount of damages that can be claimed. Here is a case where, almost inevitably, litigation will follow and lawyers should be consulted as soon as possible. None the less some notification to the seller should be made at once. Letter 4.7 is the form. The letter has been drafted to deal with the case where the goods did not conform to the description. A similar letter would apply where the complaint was of damaged goods, goods not up to sample or late delivery. Whichever it is, be brief in the description of your complaint. Leave it to your lawyer to elaborate the claim. Do, though, be sufficiently specific to identify the problem. For example, if goods were damaged, say what the damage was; if they were not up to sample, say what was the sample and what was delivered.

4.7

Accepting goods and notifying claim for damages

Dear Sirs

Our order no.

Your carrier today delivered goods under our above-numbered order.

On examining the goods we found that they did not correspond with the description in that they were [here specify what was wrong].

This is a clear breach of contract for which we shall be looking to you for the damages caused.

A further letter will be sent to you as soon as the full extent of our claim can be calculated.

Yours faithfully

DESPATCHING GOODS

A seller of goods has what the lawyers call a 'lien' on those goods for the purchase price. (See Chapter 6 for more about this.) A 'lien' means that the seller can hold on to the goods until he has been paid for them (see Appendix 1). Once, though, he delivers them to a carrier to take them to the buyer, his lien is normally lost. However, if the buyer becomes bankrupt before the goods are delivered, the seller can recover possession and stop the delivery. If there is no question of bankruptcy, once delivery is made to the carrier the ownership of the goods normally passes to the buyer.

What the seller really wants is to be sure that the ownership of the goods does not pass to the buyer until everything is in order. He wants to be paid, he wants the buyer to accept delivery and he wants the buyer to acknowledge that he has fulfilled his contract. Letter 4.8 is an attempt to achieve this. By making it clear that the delivery to the carrier is conditional, the seller is not 'unconditionally appropriating goods to the contract' (in a phrase beloved by the legal fraternity). The consignment note will contain an acknowledgement of delivery and an acceptance of the goods.

4.8

Notifying delivery

Dear Sirs

Your order no.

We are now in a position to deliver goods in satisfaction of your above-mentioned order.

Our carriers, Messrs Truck Haulage Ltd, have been instructed that they must obtain your signature to the consignment note as your agreement that the goods conform with your order. This will be a condition upon which delivery will be made. The carriers inform us that they will make the delivery on Wednesday next.

Unless we hear from you to the contrary, delivery will be made during normal business hours at your premises, Hardworkers Yard, Chingford.

Yours faithfully

SUSPENDING PRODUCTION

It was explained in Chapter 3 (page 56) that some breaches of contract gave a right to say that there had been a repudiation of the contract. If there were to be a breach of that nature before goods were ready for delivery, the seller would have the right to say, 'You are in breach and I am not going to carry on unless you make it good.' Letter 4.9 is a letter giving that message to the buyer.

4.9

Suspending production

Dear Sirs

Your order no.

We regret to see that you are now one month in arrears with the interim payment due under your above-numbered contract. These payments were fundamental to the whole transaction.

In the circumstances, unless payment is received within the next twenty-four hours all further production of the goods will be stopped. We shall endeavour to sell those goods already made and will look to you for the damages we have suffered by reason of your breach.

Yours faithfully

REFUSAL TO PROCEED WITHOUT PAYMENT

It will often happen that a customer who has a running account falls behind with payment for goods already delivered whilst other orders have been accepted from him for future delivery. Each order is a separate contract. It is not possible to say, 'Because you are in breach of your first contract with me, I am going to break my second contract with you.' They are two different contracts and two wrongs do not make a right. If you did say that, then if litigation were to take place there could be claims and counter claims. No business man wants to find himself in that position. Faced with the problem, Letter 4.10 should be sent before accepting orders from a customer who is already in arrears with his payment of overdue invoices.

4.10

To customer in arrears before accepting further orders

Dear Sirs

Your order no.

We have received your above-numbered order.

We regret to find that despite repeated reminders you have still not paid our invoices dated 23 January 1988 and 15 March 1988. In view of our long-standing business relationship, we would like to assist you by accepting this new order, but we are sure that you will understand that we cannot extend further credit. We will accept your order only on terms that no delivery will be made until we have received payment in full of the outstanding invoices, and that in this and in all future orders the goods will be despatched to you strictly on a cash on delivery basis.

Please confirm in writing that this is accepted by you.

Yours faithfully

INTEREST ON OVERDUE ACCOUNTS

There is no right to charge interest on a debt unless either the agreement under which the debt arises provided for interest or it is claimed in a writ issued to recover the debt. If a customer is continually late in paying his bill the most satisfactory solution is to change the terms of business so as to make interest payable on the overdue invoice. That means that some new contract has to be made so as to cover the old debt. Letter 4.11 is an attempt to make such a contract.

It will be remembered from Chapter 2 (page 5) that to create an enforceable contract 'consideration' is necessary. Some consideration has to be given to support the agreement to pay interest. 'Forebearing to sue' is good consideration. Letter 4.11 is, in law, an offer. It needs to be accepted, but acceptance can be by conduct. There is no need to have a written acceptance. If the customer sends his cheque for the August invoices on the basis of Letter 4.11, interest can be claimed on the old debts.

4.11

Making interest payable

Dear Sirs

Outstanding accounts

We very much regret to see that our invoices dating back to last August are still unpaid. You will know that our business terms are payment within thirty days. In common with most businesses, we cannot afford to give free credit.

The only basis upon which we are prepared to delay the commencement of legal proceedings to recover the outstanding amount is that you let us have your cheque for the August account forthwith, you agree that the balance of the accounts outstanding will carry interest at the rate of 15 per cent per annum from thirty days after their date until payment, and that you discharge the remaining accounts within two months.

Yours faithfully

MAKING A SALE SUBJECT TO A RESERVATION OF TITLE

Many companies include in their conditions of sale a clause which is designed to allow them to recover the goods if they are not paid for, or if they have been sold by the customer, to enable them to recover the proceeds of the re-sale.

The law on the point is complicated and has been considered by several High Court cases. If a company sells goods and either does not use standard conditions of sale, or has standard conditions but does not include a retention of title clause, it is possible to cover the point in a letter accompanying the goods. Letter 4.12 is the one to write.

The points that are important are, first, the reservation must make clear that it is the *legal* title that is being retained. One case fell down because the expression used was 'equitable and beneficial ownership' and that is not good enough. In law you can have legal ownership, whilst someone else has equitable ownership. (This is really too technical to explain in this sort of work.)

Secondly, the letter should give the seller of the goods, who is claiming to be the true owner, the right to enter the customer's property to recover the goods. Without this a claim could possibly be made in trespass when an attempt is made to recover the goods.

Thirdly, if the goods are going to be used by the customer to make some other product (for example, leather sold to a handbag maker), once they have been used in that way the ownership may be lost. The law is complicated and cannot really be summarised in a short paragraph. If the goods are used in some manufactured product or built into a building it is safest to regard the protection of the clause as lost.

Whenever goods are sold on a reservation of title basis the consignment should be clearly marked with some form of identification linking it to the invoice. More often than not the troubles arise when the

4.12

Reserving title on a sale

Dear Sirs

Our invoice no.

The goods referred to in the above invoice have been despatched today. The container is marked with the invoice number and the words 'Goods from Brass Stockholders Ltd'. These goods have been despatched on the condition that the legal ownership of them remains ours until such time as you have paid for them in full. Until they have been paid for, they must not be used for your business of manufacturing brass candlesticks, nor may they be resold by you. If they are not paid for within sixty days, we shall have the right to enter upon your premises to take them back, and so long as they are unpaid for you must take proper care of them, and see that they are kept separate in your stores from your own goods.

Yours faithfully

customer goes into bankruptcy. The trustee in bankruptcy, liquidator or receiver, whichever it is, will try to seize all the goods on the premises. If you can point to goods that are clearly identified as yours, you can stop him.

5

MAKING AND RECEIVING CLAIMS

NOTIFYING INSURERS

There are untold dangers lying in wait for the business man trying to prosecute a claim without the help of a lawyer. On the other hand, laying a good foundation for the claim before the lawyer is instructed can pay dividends (and reduce costs). Who knows, a well-timed and well-phrased letter may produce a settlement without the need for litigation.

Always first think, 'Am I insured against this?' If there is an insurance policy that covers the claim that is being made (whether it is a claim being made against you or one that you want to make yourself), the insurance company must be brought into the picture straightaway and no action taken without their agreement. To do otherwise will risk the loss of the insurance cover.

Letter 5.1 is a letter notifying insurers of a claim being made for an alleged defect in some product which has been supplied. It is safest to notify the insurers direct. Most businesses will employ brokers for their insurance needs. The broker is usually the agent for the business or person who is insured, he is not the agent of the insurance company for the purposes of receiving notices. Therefore giving notice to the broker will not automatically be giving notice to the company. Every human being is liable to error. Even the finest brokers can, through human error, make a mistake. By introducing one more barrier between yourself and the insurance company, you introduce one more person who may make a mistake. Send to the insurers copies of all relevant documents and correspondence. (Make sure that they are copies and not the originals.) The sort of letter that you may wish to write is set out on page 103.

5.1

To insurers notifying a claim

Dear Sirs

Re: Policy number

We are notifying you of a possible claim under the above-numbered policy and enclose for you copies of the relevant order, consignment note, our conditions of trade and the letter raising the claim.

The facts which give rise to the claim are ... [here set out briefly the facts of the matter].

For obvious commercial reasons we wish to dispose of this claim without recourse to litigation, and would like to send to the customer a letter, of which the enclosed is a draft.* Could we please have your comments.

Yours faithfully

* See Letter 5.3.

BREACH OF CONTRACT

When a contract has been broken there can be rights as explained in Chapter 3 (page 56) to regard the whole contract as ended. There can also be rights to claim damages, or rights to apply to the court for other remedies such as injunctions. Care has to be taken not to do something that will restrict freedom of action. For example, if the immediate response was to claim that the contract was at an end and seek damages, that might mean that other and more valuable rights or advantages under the contract would be lost.

The safest and surest way when faced with this problem must be to take immediate advice from the lawyer. Meantime, whilst that advice is being sought, some action must be taken to preserve the position. The answers to the questions that the breach raises may not be simple to find. They may need some time for the full effects to be felt, the legal issues raised may be complicated, and an opinion may have to be taken from counsel. The alternatives that are offered may produce some difficult choices. Letter 5.2 will gain time without pre-empting a course of action that the lawyer recommends.

5.2

Complaining of breach and keeping open all rights

Dear Sirs

Your continued failure to call off the third instalment of the goods under our agreement of 1 April 1988 is a clear breach of the terms of that agreement.

We intend to pursue our rights, through the courts if necessary. With this in mind, we are consulting our lawyers from whom you will be hearing in due course.

Yours faithfully

ANSWERING A CLAIM IN A CONCILIATORY MANNER

What if the boot is on the other foot? A claim is received and although it is disputed, commercial considerations dictate that it should be dealt with in a conciliatory manner. How should you respond? The point is made above that if there is any question of insurance involved, then the insurers must be notified. What sort of letter would be enclosed with Letter 5.1? Letter 5.3 is a suggestion. Of course, it is impossible to draft a letter that fits all facts. The important point to note is the heading to the letter with the words 'Without prejudice'. These words should always be used when litigation is contemplated and some negotiations are taking place with a view to arriving at a compromise. Later in this chapter (page 104) the effect of the expression 'without prejudice' is explained.

5.3

Answering a claim in a conciliatory manner

Dear Sirs

We have received your letter of 2 August and are very sorry to hear that you consider that the goods we have supplied are defective. We would ask that you allow us to inspect them either at your premises or here.

Every care is taken by us in the manufacture of this product, and the most stringent quality control inspections are made. If it should be that a mistake has occurred we will, of course, replace the goods without any charge to you.

We have noted your claim that in addition to a replacement of the goods, we should compensate you for the additional losses you say you have suffered. We draw your attention to our conditions of sale and particularly to condition 12 which limits our liability to replacement. However, we would not want any customer to feel that he is being treated unfairly or to have any sense of grievance. We suggest that when we have been able to inspect the goods we meet and see whether some compromise can be reached.

Yours faithfully

'WITHOUT PREJUDICE' NEGOTIATIONS

When litigation is contemplated, the parties will often want to try to negotiate a settlement of their differences. If everything that was said or done during the course of the negotiations could afterwards be used in the litigation, they would be afraid to do or say anything in case negotiations broke down. As a result the rule has been evolved that if, in contemplation of litigation, parties negotiate 'without prejudice' anything said or written cannot be referred to in the litigation if negotiations break down.

Notice two things: firstly, the expression only applies where litigation is in contemplation ('in contemplation', not necessarily actually commenced); secondly, the restriction only applies in that litigation. If, in an attempt to settle the dispute, one party makes an offer to the other which is accepted, that is a new contract. If there is a dispute about that new contract, the letter containing the offer can be used, even though it was written 'without prejudice'. The reason is that it is being used in different litigation; not the litigation that was in contemplation when the letter was written.

Letter 5.4 is a letter written 'without prejudice' and settling a dispute. If the offer contained in that letter is accepted that will be a binding contract.

Suppose that for some reason the customer who received that letter later changed his mind and wanted to go on with the litigation, he could be stopped. It would be a good defence that the action had been settled and the letter could be used to show that there was a new arrangement.

5.4

Settling a claim 'without prejudice'

Dear Sirs

Dear Sirs

Re: Claim for defective goods

Following our discussions on your above-mentioned claim we confirm that we have made the following offer.

1 We will replace the goods forthwith at no cost to you.
2 We will pay the fees of the expert you engaged to advise you on the condition of the goods and their fitness for the purpose for which you had purchased them.
3 We will pay the sum of £1,000 as an *ex gratia* payment and by way of recognition of the inconvenience you have suffered.
4 You will accept this offer in full and final settlement of any claim you may have against us arising out of or incidental to this consignment.

If this offer is accepted, please sign and return the carbon copy of this letter and we will let you have our cheque to cover items 2 and 3 by return.

Yours faithfully

RESISTING A CLAIM MADE

If a claim that is made is to be rejected and the consequences of litigation faced, no question of 'without prejudice' arises. Here is a case of 'least said, soonest mended'. Do not be tempted to set out your side of the case or to dispute line by line the allegations made. Write Letter 5.5 and send everything to your lawyer.

Do not forget that, if you are insured, even a rejection of a claim, such as is made in Letter 5.5, should not be made without first informing your insurance company and getting their consent. If you do not bring them in, you leave it open for them to reject the claim, assuming that at the end of the day you lost. Anyway, you would want them to bear all your costs, so they will want to be able to say what is going to happen.

5.5

Rejecting a claim

Dear Sirs

Re: Your letter of 1 August

We have received your letter of 1 August and note the claims you are raising.

We do not accept that the goods supplied were defective and do not admit that we have any liability to you.

We are passing all correspondence to our lawyers, Messrs Chadwick, Blackett & Dirac, to whom all further correspondence should be addressed.

Yours faithfully

ARBITRATION

Often there can be quite genuine differences of opinion which have to be resolved. The questions that arise out of an ordinary commercial association are many and varied. To go to law is an expensive and time-consuming experience. To give some idea of just how time-consuming it is, Chapter 16 gives an outline of the way in which a High Court action is conducted. With solicitors making their charges based upon the time that they spend, and barristers making their charges on the number of times they are consulted and appear in court, it does not need a great deal of imagination to see how expensive an action in the High Court can become.

It can be the case that arbitration is a more satisfactory way to resolve the problem, but not because it is necessarily quicker or cheaper. If the parties who are in dispute cannot crystallise their question, mistrust each other and want to argue over everything, then much the same amount of work has to go into preparing a case for an arbitrator as for a trial in court. It can be otherwise if the parties choose, because it is possible to conduct an arbitration according to whatever rules the parties can agree upon. One thing is sure, arbitration is private; court hearings are not. The dirty linen that may have to be washed can be washed and fully aired without the glare of publicity that the press might otherwise give to the matter.

Where the contract provides for arbitration, with some limited exceptions, for example, fraud, any attempt by one party to litigate can be stopped and arbitration insisted upon. Where the contract does not provide for arbitration, only if both parties agree can an arbitration take place. Letter 5.6 is an agreement to arbitrate. The important points to cover are: the name of the arbitrator, and do check with him first to see that he will act as an arbitrator (if there is no agreement on the arbitrator

5.6

Agreeing to arbitrate

Dear Sirs

Re: *Dispute*

We agree to the dispute between us being referred to an arbitrator for decision. The following terms will apply to the arbitration.

1. Mr Jack Jones of 1 New Street, Derby, shall be the arbitrator.*
2. The Rules of the London Court of Arbitration, as they apply to a domestic arbitration, shall apply.
3. The costs of the arbitration, including the liability to pay the arbitrator's fees shall be at the discretion of the arbitrator.
4. Only one expert witness per party shall be allowed.
5. The arbitration shall take place at the offices of Mr Jones.

Please sign and return the carbon of this letter to signify your agreement.

Yours faithfully

* Alternative point 1:

1. You will nominate one arbitrator, we will nominate one arbitrator and the two arbitrators will be permitted to appoint an umpire.

then the alternative paragraph at the end of the letter can be used), the rules that are to apply to the arbitration (it is best to say what rules are chosen rather than leave the Arbitration Act to apply – for a UK arbitration the Rules of the London Court of Arbitration are comprehensive and widely accepted) and, finally, the question of costs.

Notice the paragraph about expert witnesses. If the dispute is over some technical matter an expert witness will probably be essential. Experts, though, are expensive and the temptation to call several experts to attempt to persuade the arbitrator by weight of numbers must be resisted. Remember that, unlike a judge, the arbitrator that is chosen will probably be an expert himself and he can use his own experience and expertise when coming to his judgment.

DAMAGES

If there is a breach of contract there can be a right to claim compensation for losses suffered. Not everything that has been lost can be recovered. The rule is that the injured party should receive compensation for losses 'such as may fairly and reasonably be considered either as arising naturally from the breach of contract itself or such as may reasonably be supposed to have been in the contemplation of both parties at the time that they made the contract'. The words in quotation marks are taken from a House of Lords case that was decided as long ago as 1854. The principles that that case laid down have now been made part of the Sale of Goods Act.

Notice that there are alternatives; either the damages should come as a natural consequence of the breach or the damage must have been in the mind of the parties when they made the contract. This gives another guideline for those times when letters are being written to make a contract. See that the other party knows what will be the consequence for you if he breaks his part of the bargain. If there is something that one would probably not expect, then unless it is mentioned it is unlikely that a court will hold that it was something that the parties must have had in mind.

The problem most frequently crops up when there is a late delivery. First of all, does late delivery amount to a breach of contract at all? If it does, what damages can be claimed? Suppose that goods were ordered for the purposes of completing part of an export order and delivery by a set date was essential to be in time for the sailing of a ship. If the supplier of the goods knew that that was the case, then missing the boat would be in the 'contemplation' of the parties at the time of the contract. It would not be unreasonable to expect to recover the cost of flying the goods out so as to catch up with the remaining shipment. It would be

5.7

Claim for damages

Dear Sirs

Our order no.

Due to the failure of your company to deliver the goods ordered by us in the time stated in the order, we were unable to complete the shipment on SS *Export Helper*. As you will recall, when we placed the order with you we specifically made known to you that the order had to be delivered in time for us to make a shipment on this particular sailing, and that any late delivery would result in our having to incur the extra expense of flying the goods out to Sardinia.

The air freight charges which your late delivery has caused us are £10,000. We look to your company to reimburse this sum, failing which we shall place the matter into the hands of our lawyers with a view to legal proceedings being instituted for recovery of the amount.

Yours faithfully

unreasonable to claim that because the boat was missed, the export order was lost, and because the export order was lost the bank called in the overdraft and the company was forced to cease to trade.

When making a contract where there is some serious consequence of a failure, make sure that the problem is known to the other side, then if anything goes wrong, Letter 5.7 can be written.

LIQUIDATED DAMAGES

Because of the difficulty in deciding what damages may be recovered, contracts often provide for a set amount to be paid if one of the parties defaults. Here the problem is that whilst the law will permit parties to recover a sum which is a genuine attempt to calculate, in advance, the probable loss caused, any attempt to impose a penalty is illegal and cannot be recovered.

How do you know whether the sum that you are claiming as liquidated damages is a penalty or genuine damages? The test is that the sum must be 'a genuine pre-estimate of damage'. The problem arises mainly when making the contract. Letter 5.8 is a letter claiming liquidated damages. Incidentally, this is one of those cases mentioned earlier where it may be more advantageous to claim damages than to say, 'You are in fundamental breach, the contract is ended and we claim damages.' There may be more profit in keeping on with the contract and claiming damages just for the delay.

5.8

Claiming liquidated damages

Dear Sirs

Our order no.

We refer to condition 5 of our Conditions of Sale. In breach of the condition, you have not given us a date for delivery of the third instalment of the goods ordered. These goods are now manufactured and have been ready for delivery for the past two weeks.

Damages at the rate of £100 per week are being incurred. This sum will be added to the amount of our next invoice.

Yours faithfully

CLAIM FOR NOT ACCEPTING DELIVERY OF GOODS

The seller of goods has several choices to make when he has made the goods but the buyer refuses to accept them. First of all, we come again to that question referred to at the beginning of Chapter 4 as to 'the property' in the goods. If the legal ownership has passed to the buyer, the rights of the seller are to sue for the price and possibly for damages. If the ownership has not passed to the buyer, and this is more often the case in those cases where delivery has not taken place, the claim is going to be for damages.

Here the question of 'mitigation' comes up. It is the duty of anyone who has suffered damage to try to minimise the damage suffered. This is what the lawyers call 'mitigation'. In the case of a refusal to accept the goods, the seller should consider the possibility of resale. If the goods are ordinary trade or consumer goods for which there is a ready market there is little problem. The damages will be the expenses of resale, any decrease in the price of the goods on resale, and any other losses which fall within the principles explained earlier in this chapter (page 112). If the goods are special and not easily saleable or if the price for the goods has fallen in the market place there is a different situation. In the first case where the basis of the claim is that the goods are not readily saleable, the damages will be based upon the price agreed, and since there is no available market for the goods there will be little opportunity to minimise the losses. In the second case where the problem is that the market price has fallen and therefore less can be obtained on a sale, the price agreed will be the basis of the claim with credit being given for the price obtainable in the market place. Letter 5.9 is a letter claiming damages for failure to take delivery, with damages being based upon a fall in the market price.

5.9

Claiming damages for failure to take delivery

Dear Sirs

Your order no.

Yesterday we notified you that goods against your above-numbered order were ready for delivery. You informed us that because of a change in your requirements you no longer wished to receive them.

Because of the fall in the value of copper the price of these goods has fallen by 10 per cent.

In an endeavour to mitigate the loss that we have suffered by your default, we have sold the goods at the best price that could be obtained on the open market, which was £50,000.

We accordingly enclose our invoice for the amount of £6,000 made up as follows:

Agreed price	£55,000.00
Cost of resale	£ 1,000.00
	£56,000.00
Less proceeds of resale	£50,000.00
	£ 6,000.00

We trust that the unpleasantness of litigation can be avoided but, unless we receive a remittance from you for this amount, we shall be compelled to instruct our lawyers to commence proceedings for its recovery.

Yours faithfully

6

DEBT COLLECTING

FIRST APPLICATIONS

UK business men surprise their continental counterparts by the amount of credit they take. Sixty days is by no means unusual; the average seems to be in the eighties. When an account is overdue, when do you start to get tough? That is a commercial judgement. The important thing is to keep the debtor under pressure so that your account is among the first to be paid. Letter 6.1 is the first reminder which would be sent after several 'accounts rendered'. The stage is being set to counter the professional debtor who will leave it until action is being brought to try to raise a counter claim.

If Letter 6.1 does not produce a reply, then after about fourteen days, Letter 6.2 should be written.

6.1

Reminder of outstanding account

Dear Sirs

Invoice no.

We notice that our above-numbered invoice is outstanding. Is there any query that you have in respect of the account or the goods? If there is, please let us know. In the interests of good customer relations we try to assist in any way possible where problems have arisen.

If, as we hope, there are no difficulties we look forward to receiving your remittance in settlement by return.

Yours faithfully

6.2

Second application for debt

Dear Sirs

Our invoice no.

We regret to see that we have received no reply to our letter of 1 August; neither have we received any settlement of the account.

From the lack of communication from you we can only assume that there is no question that you wish to raise over the account or the goods. We cannot, therefore, understand your failure to discharge the debt.

We are sure that you will fully understand that we cannot extend credit to this extent with present-day overheads. Our terms of trade are strictly thirty days.

Please let us have a cheque in settlement of our account without further delay.

Yours faithfully

STRONGER PRESSURE

When polite applications are ignored, the time approaches for stronger measures. The first thing to consider is whether goods are still in the company's possession. If they are, the right of 'lien' exists (see Appendix 1). Unlike a mortgage or charge, a lien does not give a right to sell the goods, unless the contract which created it gave this right expressly. Someone who has done work on goods (a garage which has carried out repairs, for example) or someone who has sold goods but not been paid for them has a right of lien. Letter 6.3 is a letter informing a debtor that the right is going to be exercised.

6.3

Retaining goods for non-payment

Dear Sirs

Our invoice no.

We regret to see that despite repeated reminders our above-mentioned account remains unpaid.

The goods in question will not be released to you until our account has been discharged in full.

We must ask you to let us have a remittance by return, failing which we shall refer the account to our lawyers for collection.

Yours faithfully

STOPPING FURTHER WORK

If the account that is outstanding relates to a continuing piece of work and not, as envisaged in Chapter 4 (page 86), to a series of separate orders, and if payment is not made in accordance with the agreement made, then Letter 6.4 is appropriate. There is no obligation to do work for which payment is being withheld, and whilst the debtor might want to assert that to stop work is itself a breach of contract there is an easy answer to such a claim: 'No pay, no hay.'

6.4

Stopping further work

Dear Sirs

Our invoice no.

Our above-numbered invoice remains unpaid despite repeated demands. All further work on the balance of your order has been stopped and will not be recommenced until payment has been received.

Yours faithfully

THREATENING LEGAL PROCEEDINGS

When all else has failed, nothing is left but legal proceedings. What actions are open to the unpaid creditor? There is the obvious step of sueing in the appropriate court. Which court is appropriate? If the claim is less than £5,000, the County Court has jurisdiction. This does not mean that you cannot issue a High Court writ for the amount but if you do, you may not get your costs or, if there is a defence raised to the claim, the High Court may (and probably will) transfer the case to the County Court. Any claim over £5,000 should go into the High Court. In Chapter 16 a brief description of the proceedings in the two courts is given.

Letter 6.5 is a letter threatening proceedings. You will wish to avoid giving the debtor a chance to argue that he should not be ordered to pay the costs of proceedings. He will have that chance if he has not been given warning that proceedings are to be issued. If you give the warning, at least your solicitor need not send the traditional 'letter before action' and can go straight to the court. The points to note are that the heading to the letter very clearly identifies the debt for which claim is being made and this is made even more clear in the first paragraph. There should be no opportunity for the debtor to say that he did not understand what the claim was all about. The debtor is also given a chance to pay and avoid the cost of proceedings.

6.5

Before action is brought

Dear Sirs

Our invoice no.

Our invoice for £5,000 for the goods sold to you on 1 August last and delivered to you on the same date remains outstanding.

Unless payment is received within seven days, proceedings for recovery of the amount due will be commenced without further notice to you.

Yours faithfully

BANKRUPTCY

The Companies Act and the new Insolvency Act provide machinery whereby instead of going through the formality of sueing and getting a judgment for the debt (which still has to be collected by further court proceedings), a creditor can take the initial steps towards putting a company into liquidation or an individual into bankruptcy. There are restrictions on this right. The debt must be for more than £750, and in both cases the demand must be in a special form. The form can be purchased from any law stationer. It would be wisest not to attempt to take advantage of this possibility without guidance from a lawyer. If, though, the creditor is absolutely confident that the debt is undisputed and no question is going to be raised by the debtor, Letter 6.6 is the letter that would be written to a limited company, Letter 6.7 the one to write to an individual.

The letter to a limited company has to be sent to its registered office. Often a company will give as its registered office the address of its accountant or lawyer. The address of its registered office should be shown on its business letter heading. If the registered office is different from the address at which it carries on its business, as well as sending the Letter 6.6 to the registered office, send an extra copy to the business address.

Do not attempt to send a statutory demand for any debt where there is any possibility of dispute over the debt. Some people are confused as to the distinction between a company (which is a separate legal entity and is quite separate in law from its directors and shareholders) and a firm (which is merely a collection of individuals each of whom is personally liable for the debts of the business). Lawyers refer to a company when they are dealing with a limited company (either 'Ltd' or 'Plc'). By a 'firm' they mean some business that is being carried on without registering it

6.6

To a company making statutory demand for a debt

Dear Sirs

Re: Our invoice no.

The debt due to us for £5,000 under the above-mentioned invoice remains unpaid.

Pursuant to section 518 of the Companies Act 1985 we enclose a demand in the prescribed form. Please acknowledge receipt.

Yours faithfully*

---

* Where the registered office is a different address from the business address send a copy of this letter to the business address with a short covering note as follows:

We enclose a copy of a statutory demand for debt, which has been sent to your registered office.

as a limited company. It may be someone who is trading under his own name or under a business name or it may be a partnership. In either event the business is treated under the same rules as an individual. If the firm is trading under a business name, that is to say it calls itself by some name that is not the same as the proprietors, it would be usual to address formal letters to the owners as 'John Smith and William Brown, trading as The Coffee Shop'.

Non-compliance with a statutory demand is an act of insolvency and can be followed by a petition to the court for winding up (in the case of a limited company) or bankruptcy for an individual. Whether or not the creditor is willing to go to that extreme is, of course, a matter for the creditor to decide. It is not only the creditor who serves the notice who can take action. Once the act of insolvency has occurred, any creditor can take action. It is, as will be seen, a very serious matter.

6.7

Statutory demand for debt from an individual

Dear Sirs

Our invoice no.

We enclose herewith a statutory demand for debt pursuant to the Insolvency Act 1986 and the rules made thereunder.

Please acknowledge receipt.

Yours faithfully

RESISTING A CLAIM FOR DEBT

What happens when you are the debtor? If there is no defence to the claim, do not try to avoid payment by raising exaggerated claims. If your actions result in litigation you have two penalties to face. Firstly, once proceedings are commenced the liability for costs arises. Secondly, whilst interest cannot ordinarily be claimed on a debt (see Chapter 4, page 92) once a court action has been started, interest can be claimed and it will run until the debt is recovered. The result can be that credit is being purchased at a very high price.

The better course is to try to come to some arrangement with the creditor. Make an offer that might be accepted. Letter 6.8 is a letter making an offer to pay by instalments. Notice that the offer is made 'without prejudice'. This keeps the door open to argue if action is brought and either the debt is going to be challenged (who knows, they may make a mistake in their action) or some different offer is made through the court. In court proceedings it is possible for a judgment to be made for payment by instalments.

6.8

Making an offer of payment

Dear Sirs

Your invoice no.

We apologise to you for the delay in discharging your account.

Because of matters with which you are not concerned we are in the embarrassing position of having to ask for your help and consideration.

We would be grateful if you would allow us to discharge the liability to you by equal monthly payments of £1,000, the first payable forthwith and the remainder on the 5th of each month.

As a token of our good faith, we enclose herewith our cheque for the first instalment and post-dated cheques for the remainder.

We do hope that you will be able to see your way to accept this offer. We are grateful to you for your past indulgence and repeat our apologies for our failure.

Yours faithfully

DISPUTING LIABILITY FOR A DEBT

If the debt is genuinely under dispute, any claim made must be rejected as quickly as possible. If the matter comes to court all the correspondence will be looked at and if there are claims left unanswered, suggestions will be made that there was no answer to be made and that the claim is justified. What is more, the claimant must be made very aware that there is a dispute. No risk can be accepted that a statutory demand for debt be served.

Letter 6.9 should be written. Notice that it is not written 'without prejudice'. If any action is brought then this letter will be needed. In the second paragraph some explanation, albeit a brief one, should be given as to why the debt is not due. If there is any question that could be raised that there is any existing contract it should be dealt with and any counter claim should be mentioned. All this will lay the foundations for your defence if the matter comes to court. Having written that letter, consult your lawyer immediately.

6.9

Answering a claim for an alleged debt

Dear Sirs

Your invoice no.

We have received your above-numbered invoice.

May we make it clear to you at once that we do not owe the sum claimed or any other amount. Your invoice alleges that we owe you £5,000 for goods which you claim to have delivered to us. We can only conclude that this relates to the goods we ordered from you but which, when your carrier attempted to effect a delivery to us, we found did not correspond with the sample previously supplied and we refused to accept them.

Any attempts by you to pursue this claim will be strenuously resisted. Moreover, we consider that your failure to deliver goods in accordance with the sample was a clear breach by you and we are treating any contract that might have existed between us as at an end. We reserve our rights to claim for the losses we have suffered by reason of your breach.

Yours faithfully

7

AGENTS

APPOINTING AGENTS

There is often a confusion as to the expression 'agent'. It has at least two different popular meanings. An employee can be the agent of his employer in the sense that he speaks for his employer and can, by his actions, involve his employer in legal liability. A distributor is often called an 'agent' especially in the car trade. He is neither an agent nor an employee, because he does not perform his business activities at times and in the manner that the motor company control (that is, in simple terms, the test for an employee), and he has no right to enter into contracts in the name of the motor company. He is an independent contractor with his own rights and obligations.

If the intention is to create a true agency, with all its rights and duties, a great deal of care must be taken. The agent has power to do, in the name of his principal, whatever his agency permits. An auctioneer is your agent to sell the property given for sale. You are bound by his actions. If you limited his power, for example by putting a reserve on the price at which he can sell, he cannot ignore your instructions and sell at a lower price. If he does, he is said to be acting outside the scope of his authority and could be liable to the buyer if you refused to accept the sale.

An agent does not have to be appointed in writing, word of mouth is good enough. The danger in creating an agency orally is in proving the terms on which the agent was appointed. Letter 7.1 is a letter of appointment of an agent setting out the full contract. There is need, when you get to writing a letter that is to be a final binding agreement, to try to be as specific as possible. The law will in some cases imply into a business agreement unwritten terms that make sense of the contract and give it business effect. It will not, though, make the agreement for you. It is no use saying, 'On 1 December in each year we will agree new

7.1

Appointing a sales agent

Dear

Agency appointment for northern area

Following the meeting that we had last Monday, I confirm that you are appointed our sales agent for our northern area on the following conditions.

1. Term of agreement. The appointment shall be for an initial period of three months from today's date. Thereafter the agency will continue until one of us gives three months' notice of termination. The appointment can also be terminated in any of the circumstances referred to in paragraph 7.

2. Territory. You are appointed agent for our northern territory. This covers the counties of Northumberland, Durham, Tyne and Wear, and Cumbria. In those counties we will not appoint any other agent but we will be free to make direct sales. It is the intention that you will canvass customers whose head offices are within the territory, and your commission entitlement will relate to sales made to those companies even though delivery may be requested to another part of the country. For the avoidance of any confusion you will understand that this is our usual arrangement with our agents so that you may find that other agents have made sales to customers whose head offices are in their territory whilst delivery is made to a location in yours.

3. Sales targets. You will meet sales targets of 1,000,000 units a year. If you do not achieve those targets we can, at our option, either terminate the agency, alter your commission rate or appoint another agent. On 1 December every year new targets will be agreed. If we cannot agree what is reasonable, then in default of agreement, the then current target plus 10 per cent will apply.

targets'. What happens if you cannot agree? The court will not help you. It is a legal principle that an 'agreement to agree' is no agreement at all.

In any case where there is an international element do make clear which country's law is to apply. Lawyers can have the greatest amount of fun where the choice of law is not clear, and lawyers' fun of this sort has to be paid for on a very expensive scale.

4. Commission. You will be entitled to a commission of 25 per cent of the invoiced value (exclusive of VAT) of all sales made by you. You will be responsible for all costs and expenses in connection with the agency. If, however, we mutually agree to participate in a trade exhibition we will bear the cost of the exhibition stand and display and you will bear the cost and be responsible for manning the stand.

5. Restrictions. You will not:

   (a) hold yourself out as having any right to enter into contracts in our name and will not, without our consent, accept any orders you obtain. All orders will be accepted on our standard terms and conditions and you will send to us copies of all letters that you write to customers. You will, if we request it, send to customers letters making such corrections or giving such additional information as we may require. You will be supplied by us with all necessary brochures and other sales literature and also with a copy of our current conditions of sale;

   (b) act for any of our competitors nor sell or promote the sales of any product which is in competition with our product;

   (c) either during the period of this agreement or after it has for any reason ended disclose to anyone any information concerning our business, whether that information is already known to you or shall become known to you during the time that you are acting as our agent;

   (d) after this agreement has been terminated, sell, or attempt to sell, any product which is in competition with ours to any customer of ours with whom you have been dealing during the term of the agreement.

6. Payment of commission. We will send to you a copy of all invoices rendered by us in respect of orders for sales made by you. We will also send you a copy of all delivery advice notes. This will enable you to check the progress of your sales. At the end of each month you will invoice us for the commission due to you, quoting the invoice number in respect of which you claim commission. The commission will be payable fourteen days after the receipt by us of payment of the invoice.

7. Additional right to terminate. In addition to the right of termination given in clause 1 above, we shall have the right to terminate this appointment if you become bankrupt or have published against you a statutory demand for payment of an alleged debt due

from you, or if you fail to achieve the sales target for two consecutive periods. You will have the right to terminate this appointment if we go into creditor's liquidation or if we persistently fail to make the payments of commission due to you within the agreed time.

Either of us will have the right to terminate this appointment if the other continues to be in default of any obligation for one month after written notice of complaint has been given.

8. Notices. Any notice that has to be given shall be in writing and may be sent either by ordinary pre-paid first class post or by telex or by fax. Any notice sent by post will be deemed to have been received forty-eight hours after posting unless the contrary can be proved. Any telex or fax will be deemed received on the day of transmission.

9. Dispute. Any dispute or difference between us will be referred to a single arbitrator to be appointed, if we cannot agree, by the President for the time being of the Law Society. English Law shall apply.

I do hope that this will be the start of a very happy and profitable association for us both. Will you please sign and return to me the carbon copy of this letter to confirm your acceptance of these terms.

Yours, etc.

AGENT'S AUTHORITY TO CONTRACT

If an agent enters into a contract within his authority he commits you and has no liability himself, provided that he made it clear that he was contracting as an agent. If he does not make it clear and the company with whom he is dealing is left with the impression that he is contracting on his own behalf, when they find out the true position they have a choice. They can either sue him or the company he represented. When an agent makes a sale or enters into some contract on behalf of his principal, he should for his own protection make the position clear.

Letter 7.2 is the sort of letter that would be written by a sales agent appointed under a letter like Letter 7.1. Before writing this letter, he would have confirmed with the principal that he could accept the order. He has made clear that he is only an agent and he has followed through the limitations imposed upon his authority by his letter of appointment.

7.2

Agent confirming sale

Dear

I confirm on behalf of Brass Candlesticks Ltd, whom I represent, your order for 100,000 candlesticks. I enclose for you a copy of the company's standard form of conditions of sale which will apply. You will hear from them direct as to the date of delivery.

I am very pleased indeed to have had this opportunity to meet you and hope that this will be the commencement of a long and mutually profitable association.

Yours sincerely

INFORMING A THIRD PARTY THAT AN AGENT HAS EXCEEDED HIS AUTHORITY

If an agent has exceeded his authority, the principal can choose whether to accept the position and affirm the contract made or to refuse to have anything to do with the matter. There is, though, always a risk. An agent's authority may be restricted by his appointment but that may not be so obvious to the person with whom he is dealing. If an agent is allowed to act as if he had authority or if it is usual for an agent to have the sort of authority he seemed to possess, then he is said to be 'held out' as agent and the principal will be bound. It is therefore important to see that customers know that there are limits on the agent. For this reason, the Letter 7.1 has provided that copy letters will be sent to the company. See that these make the agency position clear. If the agent oversteps the mark, Letter 7.3 should be written. This should be done at the earliest possible occasion. If a representation has been made, correct it and give the true position. If there is any risk that the customer has acted upon the representation, use the alternative paragraph that is drafted and head your letter 'Without prejudice'.

7.3

Notifying a customer that an agent has exceeded his authority

Dear Sir/Madam

It has come to our notice that our agent Mr John Smith has represented to you that our candlesticks are all mounted on wooden plinths, are manufactured from pure brass and are suitable for conversion for connection to the domestic electricity lighting circuits. None of these representations is true. The sticks that are mounted on wooden plinths are a special design which would be charged for at a special rate. The materials from which we manufacture the candlesticks is not pure brass (pure brass would be too soft for the purpose) and we could not in any circumstances agree to an adaptation to permit connection to the mains power supply. Safety considerations would make this a most unwise procedure.

Mr Smith has no authority to make representations of this nature on our behalf. He is a sales representative of this company and any special terms and conditions on any order placed with us must have been agreed by us in writing first.

We apologise most sincerely to you for these unauthorised claims. We would very much like to help you and to supply a product that suits your requirements. Our commercial director, Mr Brown, will be contacting you in the hope that we may be of assistance.*

Yours faithfully

---

* As an alternative final paragraph, where a claim could be anticipated, you could use the following:

> We apologise to you for the unfortunate situation that has been created by the unauthorised claims made for our product. We hope that you will accept that we were quite unaware that they were being made. Our commercial director, Mr F. Brown, will be contacting you in the hope that we can supply a product that would meet your special requirements.

WARNING AN AGENT WHO EXCEEDS HIS AUTHORITY

In the same way that you must inform a customer of unauthorised statements or actions by an agent, you must warn the agent. If there were to be any litigation between the principal and some third party over an agent's authority, correspondence passing between the principal and the agent on the topic would be relevant and have to be disclosed. As soon as there is any suspicion that an agent is overstepping his authority he should be written to. Do not leave it to a telephone call or some oral warning; write Letter 7.4.

7.4

Warning agent that he is exceeding his authority

Dear

It has come to my notice that you are telling customers that our goods can be adapted for use with mains electricity, that they are made from pure brass and that they are normally based upon a wooden plinth. None of these is true.

I must warn you that you have no authority to make any represen-tations about the product and that you must keep strictly to the sales instructions that we have given you. Any future repetition of this type of conduct will result in our terminating your agency.

I want you to understand the seriousness of the matter. Quite apart from the damage that you could cause to us, if without authority you make promises or give warranties you will have a personal liability to the customer for any damage caused to him. For our part, if your actions were to result in claim being made upon us, we should seek indemnity from you. In any legal proceedings, we would join you and claim against you for our indemnity and the costs incurred. So you will see that it is vital, for your own protection, that you keep well within the bounds of your authority. If at any time you want to be sure of your position, contact us at once and we will give you guidance.

I am sorry that I have had to write such a formal letter but it is best that you know clearly what our attitude is and avoid problems for the future.

Yours sincerely

AGENT'S RIGHTS AGAINST HIS PRINCIPAL

An agent has the right to claim from his principal an indemnity against claims made upon him for liabilities incurred whilst acting within the scope of his authority. If defective goods were sold, it is not unknown for the buyer to sue everyone in sight. The buyer cannot be certain that the principal is not going to deny that the agent had authority. A buyer will often be advised to sue both the principal and the agent making separate claims against both and leaving them to fight it out between themselves who is liable. An agent faced with such a situation has the right to ask his principal to indemnify him against all liability. Letter 7.5 is a letter making such a request.

7.5

Agent claiming indemnity

Dear

I have been told by Tom Brothers Ltd that the goods sold to them last month are defective and that as a result they are going to claim damages.

They have told me that they claim that the material used was an alloy and not the pure metal that they said I had promised them. I did not make any promises to them about the product and I certainly did not tell them that pure metal would be used. It seems to me that they may be trying to claim on us both.

If any claim is made on me out of this order, I will expect you to indemnify me against all liability. It seems to me that we shall have to have different solicitors because there may be a conflict of interests. I will be looking to you to give me a complete indemnity against my solicitor's fees, and I would be grateful for your confirmation that this will be done.

This is an unhappy business; between us we must see that the claim is properly met and, if possible, defeated.

Yours sincerely

CLAIM BY AGENT FOR COMMISSION

An agent's rights against his principal are fixed by his contract with the principal (another good reason for seeing that the appointment is in writing). He is only entitled to remuneration for his services as agent if the contract gives him the right, or if, even though there was no contract between them, the arrangement clearly envisaged that the agent was to receive some reward for his work. In that case the lawyers say he will be paid 'quantum meruit'. All this means is that he will be paid what the court thinks is a fair fee for the work done (see Appendix 1).

Letter 7.6 is a letter to be written by an agent recording the fact that he is acting for his principal and setting a basis of a claim for payment in the case of success. Letter 7.7 is a letter making a claim for payment. Notice that in Letter 7.6 the question of accounting is dealt with. One of the problems that arises is the problem of bad debts. Is commission payable on a bad debt or not? Trade custom may say 'No'. If you want to avoid the argument, make clear what you want to say. In a particular case that came before the court, an agreement made in the way indicated in Letter 7.6 gave the agent a right to commission on bad debts despite a trade custom to the contrary.

The other question is the question of regular accounting. An agent may know that he has had a good reception and that the customer showed great interest in the product. If, though, orders are sent directly to the principal he will not know whether or not he has earned a commission. Often it happens that orders are wrongly credited to some other salesman or may be treated as direct sales. In any litigation that takes place between a sales representative and the company he represents, the lawyers will invariably include a claim for an account of all sales made so as to check that proper credit has been given. The message is clear:from the outset arrange for a regular account and check it when it comes to see that there have not been any orders missed.

7.6

Recording agency

Dear

Sales agency

I confirm the arrangement which we have made which is that on all sales effected by me of your brass candlesticks I will be paid a commission of 2.5 per cent of the invoice value (excluding VAT).

At the end of each calendar month you will send me a statement showing the amount of the invoices rendered in the month, and you will pay me my commission at the end of the next month.

Although this recognises that your terms of business say that payment is due to you at the end of the month following the month of delivery, I will be paid commission on orders obtained irrespective of the date of payment to you.

I am very pleased to have this opportunity to work for you and hope that this will be the commencement of a long and mutually successful association.

Yours sincerely

7.7

Claiming commission earned

Dear

Sales commission

I have been checking the accounts that you have sent me against my own records. I know that the customers whose names are set out on the attached sheet have ordered from you and that you have made deliveries to them. I cannot find that any payment has been made of the commission due to me.

Can you please ask your accounts department to refer to their records and either let me have a cheque or an explanation for the non-payment. I am not aware of any reason why payment should be delayed.

Yours sincerely

MAKING A CLAIM AGAINST A PRINCIPAL

As explained earlier in this chapter (page 148), when an agent makes a contract he can create a situation where the third party has rights against both the agent and the principal. If he makes the contract and does not disclose that he is only an agent, when the customer finds out the true position he can choose whether to sue the agent or the principal. There can also be problems where someone contracts in the name of a limited company which, at the time of the contract, has not been properly formed.

It is not unusual to find that in his enthusiasm to proceed quickly a business man cannot wait for the Companies Registry to send out the Certificate of Incorporation of his new company and he signs in the company name. If he does, he does so with personal liability. The company may accept liability when it is incorporated properly but unless it does and the customer agrees, creating what the lawyers would call a novation, claim will have to be made on 'the agent'. The words are put in inverted commas because he is not truly an agent;at the time he acted there was no principal because the company had not been properly formed. In the case of the agent who did not disclose his true status, if he is a private individual and the principal is a wealthy company, claim could (and probably would) be made against the company. Once the choice is made, though, there is no going back. If the position is unclear so that it is still not certain whether the agent was acting for himself or as agent, you must keep all options open. Letter 7.8 is a letter to be written to the suspected principal. If for good reason it was decided to hold the agent liable, Letter 7.9 would be appropriate.

7.8

To undisclosed principal

Dear Sirs

Contract dated 30 April 1988

On 30 April we contracted to purchase 100 brass candlesticks. At the time, we were under the impression that Mr John Smith, with whom we were negotiating, was acting on his own account. He informed us that the candlesticks were manufactured from brass and our order was placed in reliance upon this claim.

The goods have been delivered and we now find that the literature sent with them expressly states that the goods are manufactured from some other alloy.

On our claiming against Mr Smith for the losses we have suffered through his misrepresentation, he informs us that he is only an agent for your company and that you had approved of his statements to us.

Will you please let us know by return whether Mr Smith is your agent and whether you were aware of the claims that he has been making for your product. We must make it clear that we are reserving all our rights in this matter.

Yours faithfully

7.9

Holding agent liable as principal

Dear Sirs

Contract dated 30 April 1988

We told you that when the goods ordered under the above contract were delivered we discovered that, contrary to your assurances when we placed the order, they were made of an alloy which was not brass. As we told you when we were discussing the order, any other alloy would cause us considerable expense to adapt for the display we have in mind.

We intend to pursue our remedies for the losses we will suffer. You claim that you are merely an agent for the company that manufactures and have denied any personal liability. At no time during our dealings with you have you said that you were an agent, the order we placed was placed with you in your own name, and you made no comment. It was not until we claimed upon you for the mis-statement relating to the goods that you claimed to be anything other than a principal.

We are advised that your relationship with Brass Candlesticks Ltd is no concern of ours and we intend to pursue our rights against you personally.

Yours faithfully

RELATIONSHIP BETWEEN AGENT AND PRINCIPAL

The legal relationship between an agent and his principal is a very special one, but one that it is difficult to define in simple terms. The fundamental basis of the relationship is one of loyalty. The agent owes his principal a duty of loyalty and should not allow himself to get into any transaction where his personal interests and those of his principal are in conflict. If he does he runs the risk that he may have to forgo any advantages that he may gain from the transaction. Where an agent has any dealings with his principal he has to be very careful. For example, if an estate agent wished to purchase a property from someone who had instructed him to sell it, he must act with utmost good faith and he must make full disclosure of everything that is material or which could have an influence on the client. If he were to take the property in the name of a limited company which he controlled or had an interest in, he would have to disclose it. If he did not, it could be that the sale could be set aside or any profit made by him handed over to the client.

An agent must not use information gained from his principal to make a secret profit for himself. If he does make a secret profit he can be ordered to account to his principal for the profit made. The principles applying are very similar to those that apply to trustees. Not only does the agent lose the profit he might have made, he also loses any right to remuneration he might otherwise have earned.

As an example of the sort of case that has come before the court, an agent was asked to purchase goods for his principal. He obtained a discount on the purchase price but charged the principal the full amount. He had to account for the discount. If an agent is found to be making a secret profit in this way, Letter 7.10 could be written.

7.10

To an agent claiming payment for a secret profit

Dear

We are very surprised to learn that whilst you were acting as our agent on the recent purchase you negotiated for us, you were also paid a commission by the vendor. This is quite clearly a breach of your duties towards us and calls for an explanation as to the reason why you should act in this manner.

The fact that the vendor was to pay a commission to you should have been disclosed to us. In the circumstances we consider that we are entitled to demand the payment to us of the commission paid to you. Unless we have a remittance within the next seven days our lawyers will be instructed to take the appropriate proceedings.

Yours sincerely

8

REFERENCES AND GUARANTEES

REFERENCES

Business men are frequently called upon to give references of one sort or another. They range from the reference for an ex-employee to trade references for a business associate. In each case the giver of the reference must be careful to see that he is not exposing himself to claims. Clearly, if an employee was discharged for dishonesty any reference given that suggested that the employee was of impeccable character would be wrong. Yet, if the employee had not been prosecuted for the offence any suggestions made against him might give rise to claims of defamation. (In Chapter 15 a brief outline of the law of defamation is given and it will be seen that a reference would normally attract a defence of 'privilege'. This defence can be lost where malice can be shown, and an employee who had been dismissed might well try to raise this issue.)

If he had been prosecuted any reference to an offence might be forbidden if it had been what is called a 'spent offence'. Giving a reference obliges the referee to give an honest opinion and to exercise proper care. If he fails on either of these counts he could be liable to the person to whom he gives the reference for any losses suffered. Letter 8.1 is a reference for an employee. In all the references suggested in this chapter, the last paragraph contains a disclaimer of legal liability. This should always be given but it must be understood that unless the reference is given honestly and fairly, no disclaimer will be effective. If the true position is that a bad reference has to be given it is better that Letter 8.2 be written.

8.1

Reference for an employee

Dear Sir/Madam

Re: John Smith

Mr Smith was employed by us for a period of five years, originally as a clerk in our buying department and, through promotion, rising to the position of assistant to the chief buyer. He left at his own wish on 24 May last.

Throughout his employment he was a good and conscientious worker. Although we did have occasion to complain about his time keeping, we would have no hesitation in recommending him for employment in a position comparable to that he enjoyed with us.

In accordance with the usual custom of this company we give this reference in an attempt to be helpful but on the strict basis that we accept no legal liability.

Yours faithfully

8.2

Declining to give a reference

Dear Sirs

Mr John Smith

We have received your request for a reference for Mr John Smith. We do not know whether Mr Smith invited you to refer to us in this way, but in all fairness to him we think it would be better that some other party were approached as his referee.

Mr Smith will no doubt be able to explain to you the difficulty that we have.

We regret that we are unable to be of more help to you.

Yours faithfully

TRADE REFERENCES

As with the reference for an employee, any trade reference must be given honestly. Even more care must be taken because it is clear that the person requesting the reference will be relying upon it as the basis upon which credit may be given. If the reference is given carelessly and as a result someone loses money or suffers some other loss, damages may have to be paid. On the other hand, if a bad reference is given which is either not true or which gives a false impression, there is a risk of claims being made in defamation. To say that a man has not paid his account when he has may be an indication of bad bookkeeping, computer error or a genuine dispute. None the less, if it gives the impression that he is untrustworthy, that could be a defamation. The point made above about privilege in giving a reference applies equally to trade references, but so does the point about malice. With a trade competitor it may be even more possible to raise this as an issue. To decline to give a reference without any explanation can raise what the lawyers would call an 'innuendo'. Letter 8.3 should be written to give a reference and Letter 8.4 if you decide that you would rather not.

8.3

Giving a trade reference

Dear Sirs

The Brass Candlesticks Co. Ltd

In answer to your request for a reference for the above-named company, we would say that over the past three years during which they have operated account facilities with us they have discharged their obligations faithfully and in due time. We know of nothing to their discredit.

We are giving this reference as a courtesy to a fellow trader and in an effort to be helpful. In accordance with our invariable custom, we must make it clear that we do so only on the basis that we accept no legal liabilities arising from the reference and must leave you to judge, on whatever other evidence you may acquire, whether or not to do business with the company.

Yours faithfully

8.4

Declining to give a trade reference

Dear Sirs

The Brass Candlesticks Co. Ltd

We have received your request for a trade reference for the above-named company. We regret that it is our invariable practice not to give trade references. We apologise for this unhelpful attitude and must make it clear that in taking this line we are in no way intending to suggest that the above-named company is (or is not) unworthy of confidence. On that subject, we regret that we must ask you to form an opinion on whatever other information you may obtain.

Yours faithfully

GUARANTEES

A guarantee is one of those rare exceptions in English contract law where the contract must be in writing. It is also a confusing sort of contract because quite often what a layman calls a 'guarantee', a lawyer will call an 'indemnity'. The distinction between the two is a very fine one and is difficult to explain in a short sentence. Briefly, if the obligation that is being taken is to pay up, only if the person taking the credit does not pay when called upon, that is a guarantee and must be in writing. If the obligation is to pay whether or not the person taking the credit has been called upon first and has defaulted, that is an indemnity and need not be in writing. The problem has so many difficulties it is far far better to leave it to the lawyers but if you must 'do it yourself', assume that you are involved in a guarantee and insist that the guarantor puts it in writing. Get the guarantor to sign Letter 8.5.

The point that has been made about 'giving time' in the letter is to cover the law that says that unless something like this is said, a surety (that is just another word for 'guarantor') will be released from his liability if the creditor changes the terms of the contract or gives the debtor time for payment. It is more than likely that a guarantee will be called for where the company in question has fallen behind with its payments and directors are asked for guarantees before any new orders are accepted. Then comes the problem of guaranteeing payment of the old debt. Letter 8.6 would be appropriate.

8.5

Letter of guarantee

Dear Sirs

Re: The Brass Candlesticks Co. Ltd

In consideration of your supplying goods to the above company on account terms, I hereby guarantee to you payment for all goods supplied in accordance with your normal payment terms. Any giving of time by you to the company will not release me from the obligation I have accepted under this guarantee.

Yours faithfully

8.6

Guarantee by directors of payment of past and future debts

Dear Sirs

The Brass Candlesticks Co. Ltd

In consideration of your continuing to supply goods to the above-mentioned company and in further consideration of your forebearing to sue at once for the outstanding debt of £10,000, we jointly and severally guarantee to you that the company will within twenty-eight days pay the full amount of the outstanding account and will pay for all future deliveries strictly in accordance with your normal terms of business.

It is agreed that any giving of time or any concession you may give to the company shall not release us from the liability that we have undertaken.

Yours faithfully

GIVING A GUARANTEE

The person giving a guarantee must, of course, look to his own protection. Again, it is most unwise to enter into any transaction like this without professional advice. There are, though, one or two points that can be remembered. For example, there is the point explained above about the need for writing. Then there is the case that if the debtor who is being guaranteed is allowed to vary the terms of the contract under which the debt is due, then that may well bring about the release of the guarantee. (This is the point about 'time' explained on page 176.) Lastly, the guarantee itself can have protections written into it; for example, there can be a limit on the amount involved. Letter 8.7 is a protectively drafted form of guarantee.

8.7

Protective form of guarantee

Dear Sirs

The Brass Candlesticks Co. Ltd

In consideration of your agreeing to make continued supply of goods to the above-mentioned company I hereby guarantee to you payment by the company for goods to a value of £1,000 inclusive of VAT. This guarantee is given on the following basis.

1. There will be no variation in your normal terms of business as applied on sales to the company without my written consent.
2. Before any liability arises under this guarantee you will give me seven days' notice in writing of the default by the company.
3. I will have the right to determine this guarantee at any time upon my giving to you seven days' notice in writing and making payment to you of the then outstanding amount of the company's indebtedness to you, up to a maximum of £1,000.

Yours faithfully

RIGHTS OF A GUARANTOR

When a guarantor is called upon under his guarantee he takes over all the rights that the creditor had against the debtor. If the guarantee is called upon because the debtor was in breach of contract, the guarantor takes over the right to sue for damages for the breach. If it was a debt that had to be paid, he takes the debt over and can sue for it. If he wishes to put an end to his liability he can, in some very special circumstances, call upon the debtor to pay the debt and get his release.

Before giving a guarantee, it would be prudent to have an agreement with the debtor, in writing, covering the various points upon which protection is needed. Letter 8.8 is a suggested draft. The letter, assuming that it is a private limited company that is being guaranteed, should be written to the shareholders and the directors. Each one of them should sign the copy letter accepting its terms.

If it becomes necessary to make a claim on the company because the guarantee has been called up, Letter 8.9 should be written.

8.8

Agreeing to give a guarantee

Dear Sirs

I am prepared to give a guarantee for the company to cover the liability it will have to its suppliers. The guarantee would be given on the following terms.

1. It will be limited to the sum of £1,000.
2. In the event that I am called upon to meet any liability under the guarantee you will understand that I will have the right to recover from the company. In so far as the company is unable to meet its liability to me, the directors will make good any deficiency.
3. So long as the guarantee exists, you will keep me fully informed as to the financial position of the company and will not enter into any contracts or accept any obligations without referring to me first.
4. You will inform me immediately if any creditor of the company takes action to recover his debt from the company.
5. You will ensure that all liability to the Commissioners of Inland Revenue and Customs and Excise is promptly and fully discharged.
6. I will have the right to require the company to pay its debt and procure my discharge from the guarantee and this right I can exercise at any time after the liability of the company to the suppliers exceeds £10,000 or after the period of three months from today. The right will be exercised by my giving one month's notice in writing.
7. I will have the right at any time after I have entered into the guarantee to call for a floating charge on all the assets of the company to secure the liability I will have incurred on the company's behalf. In addition, I shall have the right, if I have to meet a call on my guarantee, to call for the allotment to me of a

shareholding in the company equal to one share for each one pound I am called upon to meet and (if the number of shares so allotted will mean that I would be in a minority) such further shares as will make my total shareholding in the company 51 per cent of the total issued share capital.

If you agree to these terms will you please sign and return to me the carbon copy of this letter.

Yours faithfully

8.9

Calling for payment made under a guarantee

Dear Sirs

I have been compelled to meet the liability I entered into in guarantee-ing the debt of the company to its suppliers. The amount I have had to pay including all interest and costs was £1,000.

Unless the company reimburses me for this amount within the next seven days I shall instruct my solicitors to take all appropriate proceedings for recovery.

[I have the right under my guarantee agreement with the company to require the execution by the company of a charge on the company's assets and to require the allotment to me of shares in the company. My solicitors are instructed to pursue this right on my behalf.]*

Yours faithfully

* The words in brackets would be appropriate if an agreement in the form of Letter 8.8 had been written.

RELEASE OF A GUARANTEE

If a guarantor wishes to be released from his guarantee, he must first see
that he has discharged all his liabilities to the creditor. He can, of course,
simply write to the creditor and ask to be released. Letter 8.10 would be
the appropriate form. If circumstances have arisen which give rise to a
release in law, Letter 8.11 could be written. It cannot be overemphasised
that when this stage is reached it is better that the whole thing is left to
the lawyers. If Letter 8.11 is written, instruct solicitors straightaway. If
the position is the opposite, that is to say the creditor has received a letter
requesting a release which he is prepared to give, then Letter 8.12 is the
one.

8.10

Requesting release of a guarantee

Dear Sirs

The Brass Candlesticks Co. Ltd

I wish to be discharged from my liability to you under the guarantee given for the debts of the above-named company. Please confirm the amount, if any, due under the guarantee.

Yours faithfully

8.11

Claiming discharge by operation of law

Dear Sirs

The Brass Candlesticks Co. Ltd

It has come to my notice that, without reference to me, you have extended the time for payment of the debt due from the above company. This is contrary to my rights under the guarantee I gave of the debt.

I also learn that, without reference to me, you have made substantial variations in the contract terms that existed when the guarantee was entered into. Apart from any other considerations the alteration of contract terms is a breach of the terms upon which I gave my guarantee.

In all these circumstances, I consider myself discharged from all liability under the guarantee.

Yours faithfully

8.12

Giving discharge from a guarantee

Dear Sirs

The Brass Candlesticks Co. Ltd

We acknowledge the receipt from you of the sum of £10,000. We confirm that this is the total amount due from you under your guarantee of the above mentioned company's debts, and that accordingly you are discharged from your guarantee and from all liability to us.

Yours faithfully

9

EMPLOYMENT

WHAT IS A CONTRACT OF EMPLOYMENT?

If someone is engaged to do a job of work the question arises, is he an employee or is he an independent contractor? The building industry is very familiar with what it calls 'the lump'. It is often hard to tell on a building site which men are working for the builder as straightforward employees and which are working 'under contract'. The words 'under contract' are written in inverted commas, because even the labourer who is working directly for a boss is in fact working under a contract. It is not always realised that being employed by someone means that you have a contract with that person. Because it is so rare for that contract to be in writing, most employees really do not know exactly what are the terms of that contract.

It was to meet this point that the Contract of Employment Act was passed. This Act (which applies to all contracts of employment whether or not they are in writing) not only made some provisions apply whether or not they were part of the deal, but also made it an obligation on the employer to give his employees a written statement of the essential terms of the contract. This statement is not necessarily a full statement of all the terms of the contract, just the main terms that are to apply.

What is the difference between the two contracts? The lawyers call the first contract (the contract with the independent contractor) a contract for services. They call the other one a contract for employment. And it is very important to get it right. Give a man a contract for services and (apart from sub-contractors in the construction industry) he has the problem of NHI contributions and must look after his own taxation and VAT problems. Give him an employment contract and he is taxed under PAYE, NHI contributions must be deducted, and redundancy and employment legislation applies to him. So ask the question again, what

9.1

Offering employment

Dear

Following the interview last Monday, I am pleased to offer you the position of Chief Clerk in our buying department to commence on Monday, 1 April, next. The terms upon which you would be engaged are as follows.

1. Your duties will be to negotiate the purchase of all supplies required for the efficient running of this business. You will be responsible directly to me as the managing director. In addition to these duties you will carry out such other duties, consistent with your status as a senior employee, as I may reasonably require.
2. Your hours of work will be 9.00 a.m. to 5.30 p.m. Monday to Friday. It may from time to time become necessary for you to work additional hours, possibly involving working at weekends when a crisis occurs. These additional hours will be paid for at overtime rates.
3. Your salary will be £10,000 per annum and will be paid monthly in arrears on the 27th of each month. If the 27th falls on a Saturday or Sunday, payment will be made on the preceding Friday. All salary payments will be made by direct credit to your bank. For this purpose I would be grateful if you would let the cashier's department know the details of your bank account. If by some chance you do not have a bank account, we have arrangements with our bankers (Newbury Bank Plc) under which you may open an account and as long as your account is in credit no charges will be made. In the event that you work overtime, payment will be made on an hourly basis for each hour or part of an hour. Mondays to Fridays you will be paid at the rate of £7.50 for each hour, and at weekends and on public holidays at the rate of £10.00 for each

is the difference between the two contracts? It really does not matter what words are used. You cannot make an employment contract into a contract for services merely by calling it a contract for services. It really is a question of the reality of the arrangement. The essential features of a contract of employment are that the employee not only has a particular task to perform but his employer has the right to dictate the way in which and the time at which the work has to be done. There are other considerations as well but a specialist work on the subject will explain this better. When you are employing someone bear in mind the distinction between the two contracts. Letter 9.1 is a letter offering employment. In contrast, Letter 9.2 is a letter creating a contract for services.

hour. Salaries are reviewed annually on 30 September. There is no automatic right to an increase, salaries are reviewed to take account of the current market rates and merit both in terms of work efficiency and loyal service.

4. You will be entitled to three weeks' holiday on full pay in each holiday year, in addition to all public holidays. The holiday year is the twelve-month period commencing on 1 January in each year. Any holiday not taken in the holiday year can be carried forward for a maximum of two months after the end of the holiday year, and if not taken by then will be forfeited. No payment is made in lieu of holidays not taken. If your employment ends before you have taken your full entitlement to holiday for the holiday year then current, you will be entitled to holiday pay calculated at a rate equal to £27.40 for each day of holiday not taken. No holiday pay will be made for holidays carried over from the preceding holiday year.

5. You will be entitled to full pay during sickness less any sickness benefit you may be entitled to receive (whether or not you claim it).

6. We operate a company pension scheme in which you will be offered the opportunity to participate. Full details of the scheme can be obtained from the company secretary.

7. Your employment may be terminated (subject to the rights given to you by law) by one calendar month's notice to expire on the last day of the month.

8. If during the course of your employment you have any grievance or complaint it should in the first case be referred to me. If you are dissatisfied with my decision you have the right to refer the matter to the full board of directors. Any request to refer a matter to the board must be made in writing and given to the company secretary for inclusion on the agenda of the next board meeting. We do not have any specific disciplinary rules applicable to your employment.

9. There is one matter upon which we are most insistent. This concerns the confidentiality of your work. You will in connection with your work gain knowledge of our business, our business contacts, our procedures and many of our business secrets. It will be fundamental that at the end of your employment with us, no matter how it comes about, you will not disclose to any one and you will not make use for your own benefit or for the benefit of anyone else any of this confidential information that you acquire.

You will not take off the company's premises any records or papers which may relate to our business.

If you wish to accept this offer of employment will you please sign the copy of this letter and return it to me in the enclosed stamped addressed envelope.

I do hope that you will join us and look forward to your being with us for many years.

Yours sincerely

9.2

Appointing an independent contractor

Dear Sirs

This letter confirms my offer to you of a contract for supplying a complete buying office service for this company commencing on 1 April next. I have already explained to you the range of products we need and the service we require from a buying office. You or an organisation headed by you will provide these services upon the following terms.

1. We will make available to you office accommodation at these premises, the extent of the accommodation being limited to two rooms large enough to accommodate yourself, an assistant and two typists. No charge will be made by us for this accommodation. Your right to occupy these rooms will be on licence and will automatically terminate when this contract ends.

2. You will, at your own expense, provide such office furniture and equipment as may be necessary to enable you to carry out with maximum efficiency the service required. We will, if you require it, make available to you finance to enable you to provide this equipment, the finance to bear interest at a rate equal to that charged to us by our bankers and to be deducted monthly from the amount due to you for your fees.

3. You will be solely responsible for engaging the staff necessary to provide the service and will indemnify us against all liability to the Inland Revenue and Customs and Excise for taxation and VAT payments. Since your fee is to be paid on a cost plus basis, we will have the right to place limits upon the amount which you may charge for salaries and other expenses.

4. The manner in which the services are performed will be entirely for you to decide, but will be carried out in a good and efficient manner and so that our business is in no way impeded through lack of supplies.

5. For providing these services we will pay to you a fee which will be calculated on a cost plus 15 per cent basis, plus VAT. You will render us an account of the costs you have incurred on 1 January and 1 June in each year. Our accountants shall have full access to all your records to enable them to audit the account so rendered. We will make to you monthly payments on account of the fee at the rate of £2,000 per month commencing on 27 April next. Any overpayment that may be occasioned will be carried forward and any deficiency will be paid within seven days of the agreement of your account.

6. This agreement shall be for an initial period of three years. At the end of the third year the agreement will continue unless either party has given three months' prior written notice to the contrary. If no such notice is given either party may determine the agreement by three months' notice in writing.

7. In addition to the right of determination described in paragraph 6 we shall have the right to determine this agreement on one month's written notice if you fail to provide the service with the appropriate efficiency after we have given to you notice in writing specifying our dissatisfaction and identifying the area of complaint. We shall have the right to determine the agreement without prior notice if you fail to satisfy immediately any judgement obtained against you or if any statutory demand for payment is served or published against you.

8. There is one matter upon which we are most insistent. This concerns the confidentiality of the work. You will in providing the services gain knowledge of our business, our business contacts, our procedures and many of our business secrets. It will be fundamental that on the determination of this agreement no matter how it comes about, you will not disclose to any one and you will not make use for your own benefit or for the benefit of anyone else any of this confidential information that you acquire. You will not without my express permission take off of the company's premises any records or papers which may relate to our business. Any records or papers which I may permit to be taken will be returned next day, and whilst they are in your possession will be kept in a safe and secure place.

9. Any disputes which may arise between us out of or incidental to this agreement shall be referred to the arbitration of a single arbitrator to be appointed, in default of agreement, by the President for the time being of the Law Society of England. The

rules of the London Court of Arbitration shall apply to the arbitration.

If you agree to these terms please sign and return one copy of this letter.

Yours faithfully

DISMISSING AN EMPLOYEE

The days when an employer could just shout at an employee, 'You're fired!' have long since passed. Unless something very serious is discovered, something as serious as actually catching an employee in a criminal act concerning the business, a stately process of warnings and meetings must take place, and those warnings must be confirmed in writing. At least two letters of warning will have to be sent, and you must write him letters even though you see him every morning and speak to him many times during the day. The drill is as follows.

1.   Call him in (see that there is a witness to the discussion) and tell him what he is doing wrong and give him a chance to explain. Take a note of the meeting.
2.   Send him a copy of the notes of the meeting.
3.   If there is no improvement, write to him, tell him what he is still doing wrong and call him in for another meeting, again give him a chance to explain.
4.   If there is still no improvement, write to him telling him that you are still not satisfied and call him in again.
5.   If there is still no improvement, give him the sack.

Letter 9.3 is the first letter, Letter 9.4 the second letter, Letter 9.5 the third letter and Letter 9.6 the dismissal.

9.3

Following first meeting

Dear

I enclose, for you to keep, a copy of the notes taken at the meeting with you yesterday. If you think that there are any errors in these notes or that anything has been left out let me know at once so they can, if agreed, be amended.

I repeat to you the warning that I gave you yesterday: we are most dissatisfied with your time keeping and frequent absence from work. This cannot be allowed to continue. I hope that you will take all steps to get to the office on time and that you will have fewer occasions to absent yourself from work in the future.

Yours sincerely

9.4

Warning to employee

Dear

I am very disappointed to see that, despite the previous warnings you have been given, your time keeping has not improved and you have again, without any reasonable excuse, been away from work three times this month.

I shall be in my office at 10 a.m. tomorrow morning and will hope that you will be there to explain your continued failure.

Yours sincerely

9.5

Second formal warning

Dear

On 27 May I told you that I would give you two further months in which to demonstrate that you would keep your promise to get to work on time and attend work regularly. I warned you then that if you did not keep this promise you would be dismissed.

Despite this warning your time keeping has shown no improvement and you have without reasonable excuse been absent for three days in the last six weeks. This cannot be tolerated.

You may, if you wish, see me again tomorrow at 10 a.m. and if you wish, you may bring with you anyone you like to help you give your explanation. If there is no satisfactory explanation for your behaviour it is my intention to dismiss you.

Yours sincerely

9.6

Notice of dismissal

Dear

You have been repeatedly warned that unless your time keeping and attendance improved you would be dismissed.

There has been no satisfactory explanation from you for your behaviour and there has been no improvement in either respect.

Accordingly, I have no alternative but to terminate your employment with us. You are entitled to four weeks' notice but, in the circumstances, your employment is terminated as from today and you will be paid your accrued pay to date, your accrued holiday pay to date and four weeks' salary in lieu of notice.

A cheque for the amount due to you is enclosed.

Yours sincerely

REDUNDANCY

Whilst dismissal for reasons of conduct are restricted, when the need for an employee's services no longer exists he can be made redundant. In that event he becomes entitled to a payment calculated on a basis set out in the Government's scheme of things. Frequently these days, employers are making payments far above the statutory requirements and frequently those chosen to be made redundant are selected from volunteers. When it becomes necessary to make a man redundant there is, strictly speaking, no need for a letter of explanation. It is wise, though, to give one so as to reduce the risk that a claim will be made that it was not a true redundancy but was really a dismissal which was disguised as a redundancy. Letter 9.7 is a letter of redundancy.

9.7

Notice of redundancy

Dear

As I told you when I saw you this morning, it is with real regret that I have had to tell you that because there is no longer any work for you in this business, I have had to end your employment with us. You have been a good and loyal employee and I can only hope that the enclosed cheque which represents your final pay, accrued holiday pay, four weeks' money in lieu of notice and redundancy payment will help to tide you over until you find another position.

As you will, I am sure, have noticed yourself, trade has been falling off for some years and we have now reached the point when we have to close down part of the business, which inevitably means that the numbers required in the buying department have to be reduced. All the others in the department have been with us longer than you, so I am afraid that on the 'last in, first out' principle I have had to ask you to accept the redundancy.

You may rest assured that, if at any time you are asked for a reference, you may refer to me. I will certainly say how pleased we have always been with your work and how sorry we are that we have had to part with your services.

I repeat my sincere regret at having to take this course and wish you well for the future.

Yours sincerely

EFFECT OF CHANGE OF OWNERSHIP OF A BUSINESS

Businesses can change ownership in different ways. If the business is being conducted as a limited company ownership can change either by selling the shares in the company or by selling the goodwill and assets of the business. In the first case (selling the shares) there is no legal effect on the employees, though it is possible that the new owner of the shares may want to bring all the employees into line with those employed in other companies, in what may now be a group. This can present problems. To change a man's terms of employment can amount to a dismissal giving rise to claims. Whatever is done, whether the employees agree or not, a change means that one contract of employment comes to an end and another comes into being.

Often, when the 'take over' takes place, whether it is a share transfer or a sale of the goodwill and assets, the purchaser wants to get things into an orderly fashion and wants to transfer the employment from one company to another. This is really a case where you should leave it to your professional advisers. For the purposes of the employment legislation, transfer of employment in these circumstances would not affect the employees' rights. (The question of pension schemes and share option schemes is a little outside the scope of this work; in those cases, do not try to 'do it yourself'.) Letter 9.8 is a stock form of letter that could be sent to all employees by the purchasing company or individual. As a matter of good personnel relationships, it would be as well to address each letter separately to each employee, no matter how many there are.

9.8

To employees following take over

Dear

The ownership of the business of Brass Candlesticks Ltd has now been transferred to this company. I want to assure you that there will be no changes (except for the better) for any employee. There will be no redundancies, and no changes in your working conditions. I hope that as part of a larger organisation we will be able to offer you opportunities and working conditions that will greatly benefit you.

Our business is, for legal reasons, divided into several different companies but we try to see that all employees, no matter which company they actually work for, are treated in the same manner and have similar rights and privileges. For this reason we like to have all who are doing similar work employed under the same contract of employment. This will mean that your existing contract of employment has to be changed. I enclose the new form.

If you have any questions or difficulties over the changes, Mr Jones (the company secretary) can see you and help you. If you have no questions or objections, you need take no action. If you do have any problems, I am sure that we can resolve them but you should let Mr Jones know at once.*

May I welcome you into our group and hope that we shall have the privilege of your help for many years to come.

Yours sincerely

* Alternative paragraph 3, where the employee is being transferred to another company:

In your case we would like you to be part of the team that we have created under the company name 'Brass Candlesticks (Management Services) Ltd'. There is no change at all in the duties or conditions of work; we have just grouped together all those who, like yourself, provide a specialised duty for the business.

In consequence we do, as a legal technicality, have to end the contract that you have with Brass Candlesticks Ltd and give you a new contract with the new company. Your rights and privileges remain unaltered.

CHANGE IN CONDITIONS OF EMPLOYMENT

On a change of ownership, and often during the same ownership, it may be necessary to change the conditions of employment. If these changes are substantially different from the original conditions they will amount to an ending of the original employment and the start of a new one. (This does not alter employees' rights; the new employment is treated by the employment legislation as a 'continuous employment' with the original.) The employee does have the right to object, and if he does the change will operate as a dismissal with all the consequences that that involves.

The Act does not say that employers must give the employees written notice of the changes. You can, if you like, call a works meeting and tell them all what is going to happen. It may be good management to do this and give all employees the chance to ask questions, but with no written record it does leave the way open for doubts and difficulties for the future. Better for all that a written statement is sent to the employees concerned. Again, only for management reasons, it would be better to address each letter individually. Letter 9.9 is the suggested letter.

9.9

Notifying change in conditions of employment

Dear

We have found that the old conditions of employment under which you were employed need to be brought up to date. We propose to bring new conditions into effect in four weeks' time, and I enclose for you a copy of the new conditions.

We believe that these new conditions do not make any changes that are controversial. They mainly relate to the changes that have effectively taken place already, such as the fact that we no longer pay wages in cash but by credit transfer, and that we have moved offices since you joined us. There is a change in the provisions relating to pensions; this has been made necessary by the changes in the law that have taken place.*

If you have any questions or objections to any of these new conditions, please discuss them with Mr Jones. We hope that you will understand the necessity for them and we are sure that we can solve any problems that they create.

Yours sincerely

* Alternative to paragraph 2 where the changes are being made by a purchaser to bring the company taken over into line with all others in the group:

These changes are being made so as to bring the employees of Brass Candlesticks Ltd onto the same terms as all the other employees in this group. We do not think that any of the changes are controversial, indeed we think that some of them are a distinct improvement on the old terms. We hope that they are easy to understand and are self-explanatory.

WAGES

It is unlawful for an employer to make any deductions from wages that are not authorised by an Act of Parliament. He can, for example, deduct PAYE or social security contributions. On the other hand, he cannot deduct fines for bad work or damage to the employer's property unless there is a contract to that effect between the employer and employee, and that contract is actually signed by the employee. With each payment of wages the employer must give a written statement of deductions made.

One of the deductions that are permitted is a deduction made under an order of the court which orders earnings to be 'attached' for payment of a debt or maintenance due from the employee. That order normally orders payment to be made directly to the court office. When such an order is received the employer must comply with it, he must inform the employee of the deduction and he must tell the court if the employee leaves the employment. (Obviously, if an employer is served with an order and is not employing the debtor anyway, he must tell the court that he is not the employer.)

If required by the court, the employer must give the court a statement of earnings and anticipated earnings and if a new employee is taken on and it is known that there is an order on a previous employer to make payments to the court, he must tell the court that he is now the employer and say what are the employee's earnings and expected earnings. Letter 9.10 is a letter to an employee notifying him of deductions and Letter 9.11 is a letter to the court responding to an attachment of earnings order. Letter 9.12 is a letter from a new employer to the court telling the court that an individual against whom there is an attachment of earnings order is being employed.

9.10

To an employee notifying deductions

Dear

I have received from Oxfordshire County Court an order that we must deduct from your pay the weekly sum of £15 in respect of a maintenance order made in favour of your former wife. As a result of this order the following amounts will be deducted in future from your pay.

1. PAYE and social security contributions as appropriate.
2. £15 pursuant to the court order.
3. £10 under the agreement you signed for the tools supplied to you.

Yours sincerely

9.11

To the court notifying ending of employment

The Chief Clerk
Oxfordshire County Court
Court Offices
Oxford
OXON

Dear Sir

John Smith, attachment of earnings order no. 12334

We have to inform you that the above-named debtor against whom the above-quoted attachment of earnings order was made ceased to be employed by us on Friday of last week, 13 June.

We have reason to believe that he has taken employment with the firm of Candlemakers Ltd, of 5 St John's Street, Chipping Norton.

Yours faithfully

9.12

Informing the court of employment of a debtor who is subject to an attachment of earnings order

The Chief Clerk
Oxfordshire County Court
Court Offices
Oxford
OXON

Dear Sir

John Smith, attachment of earnings order

On 16 June we employed the above-named. We understand from him that he is having to make payments to your court under an order, and that these payments were deducted from his weekly wages by his previous employer and sent to you.

The weekly wages of Smith are £250 which with overtime and bonuses should result in his receiving an average weekly wage of £300. From this sum there will be deductions for PAYE, social security contributions and (as is the custom in this industry) £10 for the use of tools supplied under a written agreement signed by Smith.

Please acknowledge receipt of this letter.

Yours faithfully

FEMALE EMPLOYEES

A woman has every right to be treated as an equal with her male colleagues. It is unlawful to discriminate against her in any way. In some respects she is 'more equal', particularly in the case of pregnancy. An employee who becomes pregnant has a right to the preservation of her employment, not merely during her pregnancy but also for a period of twenty-nine weeks after her confinement. She must inform her employer (and only if he specifically requests it does her information have to be in writing), at least three weeks before she leaves for her expected confinement, that she is going to be away and that she intends to return to work. (If there is no opportunity to give this advance warning, she must give it as soon as is reasonably practical.) Then she has to notify her employer seven days in advance of her actual return. She can, of course, change her mind and decide, after all, not to return.

All of this leaves an employer with a dilemma. His work must go on so he must get someone in to fill the gap. Provided that he informs the replacement in writing at the time of engaging her (or him) that the job is available only because of the absence of the permanent employee on pregnancy leave, subsequent dismissal when the permanent employee returns will not be 'unfair' and a claim for unfair dismissal (if, and only if, the return of the permanent employee is the reason for the dismissal) will not succeed.

When an employee leaves for an expected confinement she should be asked to put into writing her intention to return or not. Letter 9.13 should be written. It has been drafted in a friendly form but, of course, if such a warm note is inappropriate, it can be toned down. Letter 9.14 should be written to the new employee. Letter 9.15 should be written to the permanent employee about a fortnight before she is due to return. (Do make a diary note when she is due to return: it is twenty-nine weeks, beginning with the week of her confinement.)

9.13

To an employee leaving for pregnancy

Dear

Please accept my best hopes for your future confinement. I do hope that all goes well for you.

As you know, you have a right to return to work after your confinement, and we all hope that you will be back with us. It is going to be necessary for us to cover the work in your absence and I am sure that you will understand that we need to know what, at the moment, you hope to do. If you intend to come back after the confinement, will you please write and let me know. I will need something in writing as a record of your intention, so even though you may telephone I will still need a letter. I am sorry to have to be so formal but this is one of those times when formality is essential.

I will await hearing from you and in the meantime send the best wishes of us all.

Yours sincerely

9.14

On engaging a replacement for an employee absent on pregnancy leave

Dear

I confirm the offer made to you of employment as secretary to our company secretary on the terms discussed and set out in the enclosed memorandum.

The vacancy has occurred because of the absence, on pregnancy leave, of Mr Jones's permanent secretary. She has expressed an intention to return to work at the end of her confinement and if she does return in accordance with this intention, I fear that there will be no other position to offer to you and your engagement will then be terminated.

I look forward to seeing you on Monday morning if you accept this offer.

Yours sincerely

9.15

To returning employee after confinement

Dear

Can you please confirm to me, in writing, whether you will be returning to work on Monday week. I have to give your stand-in appropriate notice if you are coming back.

I hope all continues to be well with you and await hearing from you.

Yours sincerely

COMPETITION FROM EX-EMPLOYEE

The fact that employment has ended does not mean that the ex-employee is free from all obligations to his former employer. The recent and highly publicised litigation between the government and a former member of the security services has highlighted only one of the many ways in which conflict can arise. The most usual problem stems from actions taken by former employees to deal with customers of the business or to make use of information they have obtained.

Every employee has a duty to serve his employer faithfully and not to act against his employer's interests. He has a duty to keep confidential all the business secrets of his employer, and these include, for example, his employer's customer lists, pricing policy, supplier's terms, as well as the actual manufacturing process or business systems. These secrets must be kept, not only during the employment but also after he has left the employment. Letter 9.16 is a letter that could be written to an ex-employee who was making wrong use of the information he should be keeping secret.

It is important to realise that some information gained will be part of the skill that a workman gains from doing his work. Having learned how to perform a task, a man cannot be stopped from using that skill to earn his living. He can, though, be stopped from using that skill so as to compete unfairly. The technical salesman may learn the intricacies of designing a system; that knowledge becomes part of his own skill which he is free to exploit. He must not, though, go to a competitor and disclose the prospective purchasers of systems which he has learned about because of his employment, nor use the knowledge of the price charged by his former employer to enable a competitor to undercut.

9.16

To ex-employee who is using trade information

Dear

We have discovered that you are using our customer and pricing list to call on our customers and solicit orders from them. One customer has told us that you made unfair comparisons between our product and the candlesticks made by your present employers. More than that, he tells us that you told him of our prices and offered to give him a discount on those prices.

Unless (a) you return to us immediately all copies that you have that list customers of ours, and all papers in your possession relating to our prices, and (b) you give us your undertaking that you will not in future make use of the knowledge that you have of our customers and pricing, we shall make an immediate application to the court and in those proceedings we shall claim an injunction, damages and costs.

Please let us hear from you.

Yours sincerely

10

COMPETITION

AGREEMENTS NOT TO COMPETE

It is very usual to find in an employment contract, particularly in directors' service agreements (remember that a director may also be an employee, even if he also happens to own all the shares), a clause that says something like the following.

The employee will not either for himself or for any other person, firm or company for a period of three years from the date of the determination of the employment:

(a) be engaged directly or indirectly in any business competing with the employer which is situated within a radius of five miles from the business premises of the employer;
(b) solicit, interfere with or attempt to entice away from the employer any person who was at the date of termination of the employment in the employment of the employer;
(c) directly or indirectly interfere with the continuance of supplies to the employer from any person firm or company who shall have been supplying components materials or services to the employer during the year preceding the termination of the employment.

A clause very similar in effect usually appears in agreements appointing agents and it also comes into agreements when a business is sold. The seller is asked to give the same sort of agreement.

This clause gives rise to two different sets of problems. Clause (a) is a clause which, in the words of lawyers, is 'in restraint of trade' and that causes one of the most difficult problems. Clauses (b) and (c) are aimed at the duty to act faithfully to an employer even after the employment has ended. That raises the questions discussed in Chapter 9 under 'Competition from ex-employee' (page 234).

The contracts in restraint of trade start from the problem that in law they are considered to be unlawful unless they are fairly and reasonably needed for the protection of the employer's business or, where it is used in a contract of sale of a business, that it is necessary to ensure that the purchaser is not deprived of the benefit of his purchase. In both cases the obligation rests on the one who is seeking to rely on the clause to justify its use.

The court starts from the position that the clause is unenforceable and it is for whoever wants to say otherwise to prove it. How does he do this? He must show that the clause goes no further than is reasonable and that without it the business will be faced with unfair competition. The court is more relaxed in the case of a sale of a business than it is with an employee or agent. In both cases, the restriction on disclosing trade secrets will almost certainly be upheld; so, but less certainly, will be the restriction on attracting away other employees.

To justify the restriction on competition it must be shown that the area over which it is to operate is reasonable as is the length of time it is to operate. Take a solicitor's clerk who is working for a solicitor in the City of London. To try to stop him working in the City would go beyond what could be fair. It might possibly mean that his whole skills and talents could be rendered useless. If he was a clerk working in a country town, it might be different. He could be prevented from working for another solicitor in the same town leaving him free to take up employment with a firm in a near-by town. If the area chosen was so large that it would cover an area wider than that within which the existing clientele of the practice is drawn, it would go beyond that which is necessary for the protection of the business. So it would be unenforceable for that reason.

Similarly, if the period during which it was to operate was three years, it would be possible to argue that this period is needed to give the business time to contact its clients and safeguard itself against competition. Longer than this, it might be said, was quite unnecessary. On the other hand, if the restriction was included in the sale of the solicitor's practice, it would not be unreasonable to prevent his opening up a new office in the area, even if the area was as specialised as the City of London. He has sold his business and he must not take away from his purchaser the benefit of the purchase.

Letter 10.1 is a letter to write to an ex-employee who is breaking his agreement against competition. Letter 10.2 is a letter written to the seller of a business who attempts to do the same thing. Again, warning must be given that this is a highly technical area of the law and advice should be taken urgently. It is no time to try to be your own lawyer. The letter is drafted with this thought in mind.

10.1

To ex-employee in breach of contract against competition

Dear

It has come to our notice that, in breach of your agreement with us, you are calling on customers in Huntingdon. We remind you of your agreement with us which included a term that for a period of three years from the end of your employment with us you would not compete with us within a radius of five miles of these premises. You are breaking this agreement.

Unless we have your written undertaking that you will abide by the terms of your agreement (and we remind you that this term of the agreement is still effective even though you have left our employment) and will stop all attempts to sell to customers in this area, we shall instruct our solicitors to commence proceedings against you.

Yours sincerely

INDUCING A BREACH OF CONTRACT

Clearly, if a contract exists between two people both are bound by it, and for one to break the contract will give rise to a claim. In the same way, to persuade someone to break his contract is wrong and will give rise to a claim as well. It was on this basis that the trade unions found themselves in trouble at the turn of the century. When an employee stops work and refuses to obey the lawful orders of his employer, he is breaking his contract. If his trade union encouraged him to do this, the union was liable to the employer for damages. Parliament passed an act to protect the unions against these claims (recent legislation has removed some of their protection but a lawful strike is still protected) but only trade unions have the protection.

So, if a competitor persuaded an employee to quit his job, without notice, that could give rise to a claim. If a competitor tried to persuade a supplier to stop supplies he had contracted to make, that would give rise to a claim. Any attempt to persuade someone to break his contract gives rise to a claim. The most usual case that is met is where a manager, or group of managers, go off to start a rival business and persuade other employees to join them. That is the time to look at the employment contracts to see whether any of the departing employees are in breach. If they are (or if any other case of an induced breach of contract is suffered), Letter 10.2 is the one to write. Here is another case where professional help will be essential. Least said the better, but in paragraph 1 say who has broken his contract; then go on with the second sentence of the letter.

10.2

Complaining of an induced breach of contract

Dear

In breach of his contract with us, John Smith has left his employment and has joined the organisation that you have established. From information that has reached us we have satisfied ourselves that it was at your instigation and with your encouragement and support that he took this action.

We have suffered damage from this breach and we are immediately instructing our solicitors to take the appropriate proceedings.

Yours faithfully

PASSING OFF

Just as it is wrong to try to interfere with another man's business by persuading others to break their contracts with him, so it is wrong to interfere with his business by copying his goods and passing them off as if they had come from him. It is not only the blatant copy that is wrong; any product that is produced (innocently or not) that could be confused with another company's product can be the subject of an action. Actions of this nature can give rise to considerable difficulties. The question that has to be settled is, 'Are these two products sufficiently alike to cause confusion and mislead a purchaser into thinking he is buying the goods of Company A when they are really the goods of Company B?' Where the production is innocent and much time and expense has been involved in packaging and promotion, a fight is almost inevitable. When first you become aware of the problem, you must move quickly. Time lost will tell against you in any litigation. You will need an injunction. That is what lawyers call an 'equitable remedy' and it is an old legal maxim that 'delay defeats equities'. Letter 10.3 should be written, and the matter sent over to the solicitor.

10.3

Complaining of a passing off

Dear Sirs

We have seen your recent sales promotion for 'the new brass candlestick' and we have inspected the product that you are selling.

This company has for many years past been the manufacturer of brass candlesticks and has become known under its name 'Brass Candlesticks Ltd' as the leading supplier.

Considerable confusion will be caused in the trade by your use of the expression 'the new brass candlestick'. Indeed, several of our customers have already approached us to enquire why we had not informed them that we were to put a new product on the market. Clearly, your product is being identified as ours.

We must ask you forthwith to cease using the trade description 'the new brass candlestick' and to give publicity, as extensive as that that you have already given to your product, to the fact that you are not connected with this business and that your product is not to be confused with ours.

Yours faithfully

INFRINGEMENT OF TRADE MARK, PATENT, COPYRIGHT OR REGISTERED DESIGN

One of the difficulties in making a passing off claim is that of proving that you have any special right to be protected. The use of a name or the get-up of the packaging may be suggestive of someone else's product, but if they have protected their position by registration they are in a stronger position. Trade marks, patents, designs, can be registered. There is no registry of copyright, although it is possible to record a copyright with the Scriveners Company in London. If your right is being infringed, write Letter 10.4 at once. Paragraph 1 sets out the breach. In this case an infringement of patent has been chosen. If it were trade mark, design or copyright then alter the paragraph accordingly. In the same way, in paragraph 2, make the claim of ownership of the right, then call for the undertaking not to continue the infringement and the undertaking as to damages.

10.4

Complaining of infringement of patent

Dear Sirs

We have obtained one of the candlesticks that you are selling under your name 'The New Stick'. We find that it is made from the same materials, to the same design as ours and, more seriously, includes our patent insulating process.

We are the holders of patent number 12334 issued to us on 1 April 1980 from the patent office in London. Unless you withdraw from sale all products using our patented method, undertake with us not to continue to infringe our rights, and pay to us damages for the infringement, we shall instruct our solicitors to commence the appropriate proceedings.

Yours faithfully

SLANDER OF GOODS

There is nothing wrong in saying, 'My goods are better than your goods.' Comparative advertising is forbidden in some countries, but it is quite permissible in the United Kingdom. What is not permitted is knowingly to make false statements about the goods of another. That is called 'slander of goods' and it gives rise to a cause of action. In that action you must prove that you have suffered special damage. Faced with this, Letter 10.5 should be written. Start by outlining the complaint; then explain the special damage; then call for the undertaking.

10.5

Complaining of a slander of goods

Dear Sirs

We were very surprised to be told by Large Wholesalers Plc that you had told them that our candlesticks were not made of brass, and that the insulation was so defective that we had received repeated claims from customers, one of whom had suffered serious injury by reason of the defective product.

You have been familiar with our product for many years and will be well aware that these statements are completely and utterly untrue.

As a result of the information you gave them, Large Wholesalers Plc have withdrawn the order they were placing with us and have placed their order elsewhere. As a result, we have suffered considerable loss.

We must ask that you give us an immediate undertaking that you will not repeat these falsehoods, that you will write at once (sending us a copy) to Large Wholesalers Plc telling them that the statements were false and totally without foundation. We must also call on you to pay to us damages for the injury we have suffered.

Unless this undertaking and offer to pay damages is received by return, we shall instruct our solicitors to commence proceedings without further notice to you.

Yours faithfully

COMPANY NAMES

When a limited company is formed the name chosen must not be identical to that of a company already on the register. If it is registered with a name which is too like one that is registered, the Secretary of State can require the name to be changed. He has twelve months in which to take this action (unless he considers that he was given misleading information in the first place, in which case he has longer).

The question of 'when is a name too much like another' gives rise to difficulties. Two names that are spelt differently but are pronounced the same – 'Tree Bough Ltd and Tree Bow Ltd, for example – would be 'too like'. So would names where the difference in spelling is not significant – Consult Ltd and Consolt Ltd, for example. When a name is encountered which is too like the name of your own company, two letters must be written: Letter 10.6 to the other company; Letter 10.7 to the Registrar of Companies.

10.6

Requesting a company to change its name

Dear Sirs

We have learned of the formation of your company. You will see from our letter heading that this company was incorporated with the name Brass Candlesticks Ltd. The date of incorporation was 1 April 1979.

Your company's name, Brasstoff Candlesticks Ltd, is, we think, too like ours. We have checked with the Companies Registry and find that your company was registered last month.

We are drawing the attention of the Registrar to the similarity of the names and invite you to consider taking the necessary steps to change the name of your company to one which is more distinctive.

Yours faithfully

10.7

To the Registrar of Companies complaining of similarity of names

The Registrar of Companies
Department of Trade and Industry
Companies Registration Office
Companies House
Crown Way
Maindy
Cardiff CF4 3UZ

Dear Sir

Brasstoff Candlesticks Limited

The above-named company has been recently incorporated.

As you can see from this letter head, this company was incorporated with the company number 1234566 and the name Brass Candlesticks Limited, the incorporation being in 1979.

In view of the obvious similarity of the two names, will you please consider asking the Secretary of State to exercise his power to require Brasstoff Candlesticks Ltd to change its name to a name which is not so like ours.

Yours faithfully

11

INSOLVENCY

MORATORIUM ON CLAIMS

A business faced with cash flow problems has two choices: either to cease trading or to obtain some arrangement with its creditors which will permit it to trade out of its problems. The new insolvency law has provided one route by which creditors can be asked to accept restraint and be paid out of future trading; this is the appointment of an administrative receiver.

There remains the traditional route under which all creditors are asked to agree to postpone enforcement of their rights for the time being. This entails asking for a moratorium. 'Moratorium' is merely a word that means 'authorising postponement of payments' (see Appendix 1). If a moratorium is not granted, the other remedy, administrative receiver, remains. That, though, is subject to the response of the secured creditors, probably the bank, and entails legal and other costs. Letter 11.1 is a circular letter that should be sent to all known creditors when a moratorium is sought. It is important that a statement of affairs (a simple account showing the assets and liabilities of the business) is sent, and it is helpful if some cash flow forecast can be prepared to demonstrate to the creditors that there is a good chance that if they wait they will be paid.

11.1

To creditors seeking a moratorium

Dear Sir

We regret very much that trading conditions have meant that your account remains outstanding. Although we continue to enjoy a full order book, we have suffered a serious disruption to our cash flow due to the failure of one of our principal customers, Messrs Large Wholesalers Plc.

Our accountants have prepared, and we enclose herewith, a statement of affairs showing our current position. The directors' loans have been deferred and they have agreed that so long as the company continues to trade, they will not seek to recover any part of the moneys due to them until after all creditors have been paid in full. We also enclose a cash flow forecast prepared by our accounts department showing the position as we anticipate it for the next twelve months. In this forecast we have provided for a monthly payment of £5,000 to discharge existing debts. You will see that on the basis of this forecast all existing debts should be discharged and we should resume profitable trading within the twelve months.

The object of this letter is to ask if you would agree to give a moratorium on the debt due to your company. The moratorium would be on the basis that the debt will be paid over the next twelve months, and that interest at the rate of 10 per cent would be paid on the full debt (equal to 15 per cent when the repayments are taken into account). A similar letter is being sent to all creditors.

If you are willing to agree will you please sign and return in the enclosed stamped and addressed envelope one copy of this letter. Your agreement will be on the condition that not less than 90 per cent in value of the other creditors agree also.

Yours faithfully

LETTER TO LIQUIDATOR OR TRUSTEE IN BANKRUPTCY GIVING NOTICE OF CLAIM

Every day in the newspapers there appear notices under the Insolvency Act by the liquidator of some company or other asking for those who have any claim against the company that is named to give notice of their claim. When a company goes into liquidation or some individual is made bankrupt, the liquidator (in the case of a company), or the trustee (in the case of an individual), has to advertise for claims. This advertisement has to be made in the *London Gazette*, a national newspaper and a newspaper which circulates in the district in which the particular business was carried on. If you want to be sure that you see all the advertisements, you had better take the *London Gazette*.

The liquidator (to save repeating it every time, the Trustee in Bankruptcy has exactly the same duties) when he is appointed has received from the company a list of all the creditors of the company, and he has probably written to them all with a form of 'proof of debt'. There is always the case, though, of the creditor whose debt has been overlooked, or whose debt is disputed and therefore has not been included on the list.

Every responsible director should make a point of scanning the statutory advertisements. Apart from anything else opportunities can arise. More important, though, where a debtor of the company goes into liquidation, the company must put in a proof of debt. This is on a special form that will be obtained from the liquidator. When the advertisement is seen, check whether a proof of debt has already been made; if it has not, write Letter 11.2.

11.2

In response to statutory advertisement for proof of debt

Dear Sir

Large Wholesalers Plc (in liquidation)

Your notice in today's *Financial Times* for claims in the above-mentioned liquidation has been observed.

This company has a claim against Large Wholesalers Plc in the sum of £25,000. Will you please let us have the appropriate form of proof of debt for completion.

Yours faithfully

CLAIM TO OWNERSHIP OF GOODS AGAINST RECEIVER OR LIQUIDATOR

First of all, understand that there is a difference between a receiver and a liquidator or a trustee in bankruptcy. A liquidator is appointed when a company is insolvent. He may be appointed by the court or he may be appointed when the shareholders decide to cease trading. A receiver is appointed by a creditor who has a charge (which means a mortgage – in the case of a company a mortgage is often called a debenture). The company may not be insolvent. It may just be short of cash. The receiver will sell up all the assets of the company, take what he gets for them and pay off the creditor who appointed him. Then he resigns and hands the company back to the directors to carry on with the trading.

The liquidator's task is to sell up all the assets of the company and distribute all that he gets between all the creditors. The risk that a supplier runs who has supplied goods under a reservation of title (see Chapter 4, page 94), or someone who has hired goods or leased them to the company, is that his goods will be sold by the liquidator or receiver. This is why, in Chapter 4, it is emphasised that when goods are sold on a reservation of title, the consignment should be marked with some form of identification.

So as soon as any notice, formal or informal, is received that the company has suffered the appointment of a receiver or liquidator, action must be taken to recover the goods. Letter 11.3 should be written at once. Expect that the reply will be for some proof that the claim being made is correct, so have available all the invoices, correspondence and consignment notes to back up the claim. An alternative form is suggested where the claim is being made by a hirer or lessor.

11.3

To receiver claiming goods

Dear Sir

Small Wholesalers Ltd

We have seen that you have been appointed receiver of the above-named company. On the company's premises is a consignment of goods marked 'Goods from Brass Stockholders Ltd'. These goods belong to us. They were the subject of an order placed by the company of which you are the receiver, and were delivered by us under reservation of title.

No payment for the goods has been received by us and the property in them remains with us. Under the terms upon which they were delivered we have a right of entry to the company's premises to repossess our property. We propose to exercise this right on Monday next, on which day our carrier will call to collect them.

Yours faithfully*

---

* Alternative letter where the claim is made by a hirer or lessor:

We have seen that you have been appointed receiver of the above-named company. On the company's premises is [here set out whatever equipment is concerned] which is hired [leased] from us.

The agreement between us and the company provides that the agreement is automatically determined in the event that the company suffers the appointment of a receiver or liquidator.

In the circumstances, we intend to repossess the equipment and our carrier will be calling on the premises on Monday next for this purpose.

CLAIMS MADE BY A LIQUIDATOR OR RECEIVER

The duty of a receiver or a liquidator is, as explained above, to collect in all the assets of the company. This involves collecting in debts or prosecuting claims that the company may have. When a claim of this nature is faced there are three possibilities.

The claim may be admitted. In this case there is little to do but negotiate. The claim may be denied, in which case you can challenge the liquidator. (See Chapter 16 – in these circumstances a defendant has the right to require security for his costs where the plaintiff is insolvent.) The claim may be admitted but it is asserted that there is a counter claim which can be set off. (See Chapter 16, page 330, for an explanation of how a set off is dealt with as part of a defence.)

Whichever it is, a reply must be made. Where the claim is accepted Letter 6.8 with suitable modification could be written; where it is going to be resisted for one reason or another Letter 11.4 should be written.

11.4

Reply to claim by liquidator

Dear Sir

We have received your letter of 2 July. We are in no way indebted to Large Wholesalers Plc (in liquidation).

We assume that the claim relates to an order for goods which we placed in June of last year. When goods which purported to be in compliance with this order were delivered, we found that they did not correspond to the sample previously supplied and we refused to accept them.

Any attempt to pursue this claim will be strenuously resisted.

Yours faithfully*

* Alternative letter where a set off is raised:

We have received your letter of 2 July claiming for the amount of £10,000 which it is suggested is due from us to Large Wholesalers Plc (in liquidation).

We assume that the claim relates to a consignment of brass candlesticks which we purchased from the company some twelve months ago.

As we have informed the company previously, the goods proved to be defective in many respects. We had made it known to the company that they were required to fulfil a specific order from Grand Hotels Ltd. The company gave a specific warranty that the goods would be free from defect and undertook to indemnify us against all claims that might be made.

Claim has now been made upon us by Grand Hotels Ltd in the sum of £15,000, and we shall set off against any liability that there might be from us the amount of the damages we may be ordered to pay.

12

PROPERTY

NEW LEASE

When a lease is granted it is for a fixed period. It is common for it to be for seven, fourteen or twenty-one years. When that period expires, if it is a business lease, the tenant has the right to a new lease for a period not exceeding fourteen years. The landlord's right to resist this is very limited. However, if nothing is done, with no application by the tenant for a new lease and no attempt by the landlord to end the situation, the old lease carries on at the same rent and on the same terms.

So far as the tenant is concerned, in these days of ever increasing rents, it is best to say nothing. Leave it to the landlord to take the initiative. The landlord must send a notice to quit in a special form. In that form he asks the tenant to say whether or not he will give up possession at the expiry of the notice to quit. Letter 12.1 is the letter to write when that notice is received. The notice will also say whether the landlord will oppose an application for a new lease.

12.1

Tenant's answer to notice to quit served under the Landlord and Tenant Act 1954

Dear Sirs

We have received your notice to terminate our continuation tenancy of these premises.

At the expiry of the notice we will wish to retain possession and will, in due course, be making application for a new lease.

Yours faithfully

APPLYING FOR A NEW LEASE

There are two very important points to appreciate from the outset. First, get a chartered surveyor to help you as soon as possible. Negotiating a lease needs expertise and knowledge of the local property market. Second, there are strict time limits. It does not matter that the landlord has said that he will not oppose the grant of a new lease; the odds are that it will take some time for the terms to be agreed, and before that happy result has occurred the time for applying to the court for a new lease will have run out. An application will have to be made and held in abeyance whilst the negotiations continue. When Letter 12.1 has been written, get your surveyor organised and then write Letter 12.2.

12.2

Opening negotiations for a new lease

Dear Sirs

Further to our letter of 21 February, we have now instructed Mr C. Dick FRICS of the firm of C. Dick and Partners to represent us in negotiations for a new lease of these premises. He will be in touch with you in due course. Meantime, we will be continuing to pay our rent at the present rate.

Yours faithfully

IMPROVEMENTS AND ALTERATIONS

During the course of the lease there will be occasion when some alterations become necessary or desirable. Remember that most leases contain clauses that forbid any work being done without the landlord's consent. When work is being done, there are two possibilities: one is that the work is an improvement to the property, which could mean that the tenant, if he goes about it the right way, can claim compensation at the end of the lease, the other is that at the end of the lease the landlord can ask for the premises to be put back as they were.

For example, suppose it was thought necessary to divide up one floor and create additional office space. This could be done with demountable partitioning which it would be technically possible for the tenant to take away with him at the end of the term, or it could be done with some permanent construction which would enhance the letting value of the property. In either event the landlord must be asked for permission. In asking, the tenant can seek a permission which will suit his plans. Letter 12.3 is a letter seeking permission for demountable partitioning which will not give any right to compensation for improvement, but will enable the tenant to take it away with him when he leaves. (In all probability, what he would do is agree to sell the partitioning either to an incoming tenant or to the landlord, and get some sort of benefit for himself at the end of the lease.)

Letter 12.4 is a letter asking for permission to carry out the same sort of work as an improvement. The test of an improvement is that it must not be merely some form of fixture which the tenant can take away at the end of the lease and that it adds to the letting value of the property.

12.3

Seeking consent to alterations not improvements

Dear Sirs

We wish to increase the office accommodation available to us in these premises, and enclose herewith a copy of a plan showing our proposals. As you can see, we wish to erect demountable partitioning in the position shown. This partitioning will be affixed to the premises in such a manner that it can be removed and taken away by us at the end of the term, without causing any damage or deterioration to the property.

Under the provisions of our lease, we would ask for your permission to have this work carried out. We would, of course, undertake that no damage would be caused to the property during the carrying out of the work and that at the end of the term of the lease we will remove the partitioning.

Yours faithfully

12.4

Requesting permission to carry out improvements

Dear Sirs

We wish to create additional office accommodation on these premises and we enclose herewith plans and a specification of the work we propose.

We believe that this will constitute an improvement to the property, and we would ask for your consent to our carrying out the work.

We will obtain all necessary building and other consents from the local authority, and will have the work carried out entirely at our own expense. We will ensure that no damage is caused to the building and will make good immediately any damage which does occur.

Please may we hear from you.

Yours faithfully

CHANGE OF USE

Leases usually contain a provision which restricts the way in which the property may be used. Maybe, for example, the property was originally used as a shop with living accommodation over it. Now downstairs is an estate agent's business and upstairs would make ideal office extension for the business. No matter that the local planning authority does not object; if the lease says that it must be used for living accommodation, the landlord must be asked for permission before there is any change. Letter 12.5 is a letter requesting permission to change use.

12.5

Requesting permission to change use

Dear Sirs

We are in need of additional office accommodation at these premises, and have spoken to the local planning officer to ascertain his view on a possible change of the use of the upper part of the premises to offices. He gives us to believe that there would be no planning objection raised.

Would you please take this letter as a formal application under the terms of our lease for permission, subject to formal planning permission being granted, to change the use of the upper floor from residential use to office use. We will undertake, at our own expense to apply for planning permission for the appropriate change of use.

We await hearing from you.

Yours faithfully

LETTER COMPLAINING TO LANDLORD

Unfortunately, from time to time landlords and tenants fall out. Often the cause is repairs. The tenant, maybe, considers that the landlord should repair some part of the building whilst the landlord either disagrees or just does not want to do anything. The one thing the tenant must not do is withhold his rent as a way to force the landlord's hand. Rent has to be paid and, if it is not, a landlord has his rights. Better by far for the tenant to lay the groundwork for a claim for compensation. Letter 12.6 is a letter of complaint.

12.6

Tenant's complaint to landlord

Dear Sir

We have from time to time complained to you and to your agents, Messrs C. Maitland & Co., about the condition of the roof at these premises.

The roof has missing tiles and the water is penetrating through into the roof space (which is not part of our lease). It then comes through our ceiling causing damage to the fabric and decorations of the part of the premises leased to us. This is causing damage, not only to the building but also to our materials and property. More than that it is creating conditions which are harmful to the health and safety of our employees.

We are taking advice as to our remedies with a view to taking proceedings to compel you to have the necessary work carried out. It is right that you should know that should the condition be allowed to continue we shall be forced to vacate that part of the premises affected by the damp. This will cause serious economic loss to our business and will involve us in the considerable expense of taking temporary premises whilst these are unusable.

Yours faithfully

COMPLAINT BY LANDLORD AGAINST HIS TENANT

It may be that the complaint is being made by the landlord against his tenant. In that case there are at least two important messages for the tenant. First, he may accept the complaint or he may not. Either way, though, he must deal with it. Accept it, reject it, but do not in any circumstances, ignore it. The second is at all costs pay the rent. A landlord who accepts rent knowing of a breach by his tenant has probably 'waived the breach' as a lawyer would say. In other words, he has released the tenant from the consequences of his misbehaviour. If the complaint is justified, there is little that can be said except, 'I am sorry and will not do it again.' If it is unjustified, Letter 12.7 can be written.

Of course, each case will depend on its own facts. The important thing is to show that you have taken serious notice of the complaint, have investigated the circumstances and done all that you can to ensure that the matter complained about is not caused by your actions (or inactions). If you can show that the problem is an unavoidable consequence of the nature of the property, then bring that out in your letter.

12.7

Tenant rejecting an alleged complaint

Dear Sir

We have received your letter in which you complain that, in breach of the terms of our lease, we are causing an obstruction to the common entranceway to these and the adjoining premises.

You have referred to one incident that is alleged to have occurred last Thursday but have not given other examples. We have carefully investigated and have asked all our drivers to see whether there is any reasonable ground upon which your complaint could be based. The incident last Thursday was caused when a delivery vehicle not owned by us arrived to make a delivery to these premises. As soon as it was apparent that an obstruction might be caused, we had the vehicle moved. We have not been able to identify any other occasion when vehicles have obstructed the access.

The problem is caused by the unfortunate layout of the properties, and despite all reasonable precautions that are taken by us and our neighbours, difficulties will from time to time arise. There is always a driver on hand and all drivers are under orders to move their vehicles away from any position which could cause obstruction.

We have dealt with your complaint at length to show the import-ance that we attach to good landlord and tenant relations and to emphasise that we wish to be as co-operative as is possible. We cannot accept that in this instance any complaint is justified.

Yours faithfully

SERVICE TENANTS

When an employee is to be given accommodation as part of his employment it is important to see that you do not create a tenancy which cannot be brought to an end with the employment. New legislation may be relaxing the protection given to tenants under the Rent Acts but there will always be the problems of lettings created under traditional common law principles. The right to accommodation must be related to the employment.

Under the Rent Acts, it was necessary to be able to show that the employee was required to live where he did 'for the better performance of his duties'. For example, a caretaker was required to live on the premises. In Chapter 9, letters creating employment are suggested. Rather than add a long section about the right to occupy property in an employment letter, Letter 12.8 should be written.

12.8

Creating a service tenancy

Dear

We have written to you a letter setting out the terms upon which you are to be employed as resident manager of our shop at Market Harborough. It will be necessary for you to reside at the premises so that you can be available to receive deliveries out of normal hours, and can provide security supervision of the premises during bank holidays and Sundays.

Your employment will include the right to occupy the premises above the shop at No. 5, The High Street. Your occupancy will be on the following terms.

1. You will pay a weekly rent (exclusive of rates) of £25.
2. You will be responsible for the rates chargeable on the property and for the expense of all gas, water and electricity consumed on the premises.
3. You will be responsible for all interior decoration and the repair of glass in the windows and maintenance of the garden ground at the rear which you will keep clean and free from weeds.
4. We will be responsible for all repairs to the roof and main structure (except for repairs made necessary by any misuse of the property caused by you, or anyone on the property with your permission) and for external decoration.
5. You will not permit anyone, other than members of your immediate family, to reside permanently on the premises.
6. You will not do or permit anything to be done which may be or become a nuisance or annoyance to the neighbours or will adversely affect the business being carried on in the shop.
7. The whole purpose of your occupancy of these premises is to enable you to fulfil your terms of employment which include the obligation to receive goods and deliveries outside of normal

trading hours and to safeguard the security of the shop premises during all times when it is not open for business.

8. This right of occupancy will cease immediately at the end of your employment (however the employment may end) and you will then vacate and give vacant possession of the property.

In acknowledgement of your acceptance of these terms will you please sign and return to me the copy of this letter which we enclose.

Yours sincerely

LICENCES TO OCCUPY

Apart from letting employees occupy part of the business property for employment reasons, it is often found necessary to let some other business occupy part of the property. Here it is important, if the property is held under a lease, to be sure that the lease will permit the proposal. Most usually it does not. If it does, or the premises are freehold, Letter 12.9 can be written. The important point is to be sure that it is a licence that is being granted and not a lease. A lease can give rights of renewal as described at the beginning of this chapter (page 266), a licence does not give the same right. The distinction is between the right to exclusive possession of the part that is being let and a right only to share occupancy.

12.9

Granting a licence to occupy

Dear

I confirm my agreement to your having a licence to occupy part of the ground floor of our warehouse premises at Back Street, Oakham. The licence is on the following terms.

1. The area you may occupy is that part of the ground floor which we shall from time to time indicate. Initially it will be the part which is demarcated by demountable partitioning. We reserve the right to share occupancy of this area or to require you to move to some other part of the ground floor having an equal area.

2. You will pay a licence rent of £2,000 per annum payable monthly in advance, plus an amount equal to 25 per cent of the rates chargeable on the whole of the premises, and 30 per cent of the charges made for gas and electricity supplied to the whole premises.

3. We will be responsible for all repairs and decorations to the premises. You will pay a share equal to 25 per cent of the total expenditure in each year of the costs of fulfilling this obligation.

4. You will not share the occupancy of the premises with any person, firm or company and will not do anything on the premises which may be or become a nuisance or annoyance to us.

5. You will not use the premises for any purpose other than that of storage of goods, and will not load the floor with loads in excess of five tons per square metre.

6. You will not obstruct our access to any part of the premises.

7. This licence will determine the following:
   (a) forthwith:
      (i) on your suffering the appointment of a receiver, or on the passing of any resolution for creditors winding up,

or if any statutory demand is made against you for
payment of any debt;

(ii) if you are in default for one month after service upon
you by us of any notice specifying a breach by you of
any of your obligations under this licence;

(iii) if any rent is due from you and unpaid for a period of
three months;

(b) by six months' notice in writing served by either of us, such
notice to expire on any day in the year.

8. Any dispute or difference between us arising out of or incidental
to this licence shall be referred to the arbitration of a single
arbitrator to be appointed (in default of agreement) by the
President for the time being of the Royal Institute of Chartered
Surveyors.

If you agree these terms will you please sign and return one copy of
this letter.

Yours sincerely

13

BANKS, SOLICITORS AND ACCOUNTANTS

DRAWING A CHEQUE ON OVERDRAFT ACCOUNT

The one thing that is common to correspondence with banks, solicitors and accountants is that you must tell them the whole story. Otherwise you will find troubles ahead. So far as a bank is concerned, before you go into overdraft see that you have cleared the arrangement with your bank manager. Tell him why you need to have the facility and then make sure that you record what you have agreed. He will have made a note in his 'log' (or whatever he chooses to call his record of interview notes). See that your record matches his. If you write and he does not honour your cheque, then you may be in a position to do something about it. Letter 13.1 is the sort of thing to write.

13.1

To a bank following agreement for a facility

Dear

I would like to thank you for the help that you agreed to give me this morning.

Just to confirm the arrangement, it was agreed that you would allow my account to be overdrawn to the extent of £10,000. This arrangement will continue for a period of three months, after which it will be reviewed. I will be charged interest at the rate of 3 per cent above the bank's base rate, and will pay an arrangement fee of £100.

Relying upon this arrangement, I have today issued a cheque for £5,000 in favour of Brass Candlesticks Limited for the first consignment of goods which I have now ordered. I hope that with the help you have given me this will be the start of a very profitable venture.

Yours sincerely

STOPPING A CHEQUE

When it becomes necessary to stop a cheque, speed is essential, as is a written record. It needs care, particularly if the result is likely to be litigation. As will be explained in more detail in Chapter 16, in litigation all relevant letters must be disclosed. This will probably mean that what you write now will be disclosed to the other side and to the court. Least said, soonest mended. Write Letter 13.2. Identify the cheque by its number and clearly indicate, again by its number, the account on which the cheque was drawn.

13.2

Stopping a cheque

Dear

I confirm my telephone call this morning when I instructed you that I did not want you to pay the cheque number 000338 drawn on my account number 33127018 at your branch. The cheque is for the sum of £5,000 and is in favour of Brass Candlesticks Limited.

I have informed the payee of the orders that I have given to you. Please will you confirm that payment will be stopped, and will you please let me know if the cheque is presented for payment.*

Yours sincerely

* If a replacement cheque is going to be issued, for example, because the original has been lost, an explanation should be given to the bank to avoid the confusion that might arise if both cheques are presented for payment. In place of the second paragraph write:

The reason that I am giving you these instructions is that the cheque has been lost. I am issuing a replacement cheque (my cheque number 000339) which will no doubt be presented to you for payment in the normal way.

LETTER TO THE BANK GIVING AUTHORITY TO DISCLOSE DETAILS OF THE ACCOUNT

There will be occasions when for one reason or another the bank is requested to disclose details of the account. Banks are correctly proud of the secrecy with which they conduct their customers' affairs. They will only disclose information on explicit and written authority. Letter 13.3 should be written when a bank is being authorised to disclose information.

13.3

Authorising a bank to disclose information

Dear

You will be hearing from Messrs Newton, Halley & Wren, chartered accountants, who will be asking you to provide them with details of my account number 33127018.

This letter gives you my permission and authority to disclose to them such information as they may request of the operation of the account from 1 January 1987 to date. You should not disclose details before that date, neither should you disclose details of my private account number 33016109.

Yours sincerely

BANKER'S REFERENCE

When a trade customer wishes to open an account, or when it is
proposed to give a tenancy or licence to occupy premises, it is customary
to request bank references. No bank will respond to a direct request for a
reference, the request must come from another bank. When a reference
of this nature is required, write to your own bank Letter 13.4. Explain
the reason for the request, give full details of the amounts involved and
give particulars of the bank of whom enquiry must be made.

13.4

Asking for a banker's reference

Dear

We are proposing to grant to Messrs Brass Candlesticks Ltd a licence to occupy part of our warehouse at Back Street, Oakham. The rent payable is £2,000 per annum, and in addition they have to bear 25 per cent of the rates, 30 per cent of the charges for gas and electricity supplied to the whole premises and 25 per cent of the annual costs of maintenance of the premises. This will mean a total annual commitment for them of approximately £3,500.

Would you please enquire of their bankers, Newbury Bank Plc of Upper Street, Newbury, whether Brass Candlesticks Ltd can be considered good for this amount.

Yours sincerely

OBTAINING A QUOTATION FROM A SOLICITOR

Until recently, the idea of asking solicitors to quote for their fees would have been impossible to contemplate. Now, in a conveyancing matter, it is becoming almost standard practice, and for other matters solicitors are encouraged by the Law Society, if not to give a firm quotation, at least to indicate their charging rate. Indeed, the Law Society has given a formal notice to the profession that a solicitor should, when requested by his client, give an estimate of the cost of acting in a particular matter and if, for some reason, he cannot give even an approximate estimate he should say so and then give such general forecast of the likely cost as he can.

In conveyancing matters the Law Society has given solicitors a form of estimate which they are encouraged to use. An estimate might be written in such a way as to bind the solicitor to the precise sum. Most solicitors, though, would be more careful and make sure that what they sent was a true 'estimate' which did not bind them to a fixed fee.

Remember that the only thing a solicitor has to sell is his knowledge and experience. That means he is selling his time. He will make a charge based upon the time he spends plus a 'mark up' to reflect various factors, including the particular complications and specialities of the matter. If you are going to instruct a solicitor in a complex commercial negotiation or a possibly difficult piece of litigation, write Letter 13.5. To enable him to give a quotation, he will need to know some of the problems he will have to face.

13.5

To solicitors asking for a quotation

Dear Sirs

I am contemplating the possibility of my company making an offer to acquire the entire share capital of an enterprise based in the Midlands. The total purchase moneys involved will be in the order of £1.5 million.

I have already negotiated the necessary financial arrangements to enable me to carry out this transaction, and now would like to give instructions to lawyers to proceed. My accountants, Messrs Newton, Halley & Wren, have recommended that I ask your firm to act for me.

Can you give me an estimate of the probable costs that I am likely to incur, including all appropriate disbursements? If you feel that in a matter of this nature your charges cannot be predicted in advance could you please give me some general idea, and also let me know the basis upon which your charges will be calculated. If they are based upon an hourly charging rate, could you let me know the amount of that charge? If you need further information to enable you to give an indication of the possible costs involved, please let me know.

Yours faithfully

MAKING A COMPLAINT TO A SOLICITOR

When it is necessary to complain about the service received from your solicitor, address your letter to the senior partner. Give him facts and particularly tell him of the individuals who have handled the matter. Again, it follows that each case will be special, but Letter 13.6 should help. Where, as in the case that is envisaged by Letter 13.6, the complaint amounts to a claim that the firm has been negligent, the reply will almost certainly be to the effect that because of the nature of the complaint you should seek other advice.

Do this as soon as possible and do not think that one solicitor will not sue another. If your solicitor practises in a small local community, it may be better to go to the nearest large town where there is a large number of solicitors to choose from. If you cannot get a recommendation to another firm, approach the Law Society for a list of names from which you can choose. The Society cannot, itself, deal with claims for negligence; its responsibility is for professional misconduct and it has no right or power to make judgment on questions that are essentially for the courts to decide. It will, though, give help to find a solicitor who will, without fear or favour, prosecute your case for you.

Letter 13.7 is a letter seeking help to make a claim for negligence. It would be wise, before writing the letter, to make contact with the partner who will be dealing with the matter. A telephone call to make contact and give an outline of the matter will help him and prepare him for action. See that he has all the papers in your possession and knows where he can see any other relevant papers that you cannot send him.

13.6

To solicitors making a complaint

Dear Mr Peace

I am writing to you as the senior partner of Peace, Haigh & Ellis.

Your Mr Manson has been conducting on my behalf a claim that I have been making against Brass Candlesticks Limited. I gave him the instructions in January 1986 and have from time to time since then seen him to give him such further information as he required.

Now, after two and a half years, I learn that he has not issued a writ, and I am told that, as six years have elapsed since the cause of my complaint arose, I am out of time and have little chance of success in any litigation.

I have, at Mr Manson's request, paid your firm on account of the costs involved £750. I am sure that I need not explain my feelings.

I would like to have an explanation from you of the reasons for the failure to protect my interest and to know from you what action you propose to take to recompense me not only for the loss I have suffered but also for the frustration, time and expense which this whole matter has involved for me.

Yours sincerely

13.7

To solicitors giving instructions in an allegation of negligence by a solicitor

Dear Sirs

Messrs Peace, Haigh & Ellis

I confirm my telephone conversation with your Mr Sutcliffe when I asked for your help to pursue my claim that Messrs Peace, Haigh & Ellis had been negligent in the handling of a claim I was making against the company Brass Candlesticks Ltd.

I enclose my complete file of correspondence. All the relevant papers regarding my claim against Brass Candlesticks Ltd are with Messrs Peace, Haigh & Ellis.

My allegation is based upon the fact that no action was taken on my behalf in two and a half years, and in consequence my claim became barred because no writ was issued within six years.

When you have had a chance to consider the file I would be pleased if you could give me an appointment so that the matter may be further considered.

Yours faithfully

OBTAINING A REMUNERATION CERTIFICATE FROM A SOLICITOR

When solicitors render their bills, they cannot just think of a number and charge it. Their costs are regulated by law. Once a bill has been sent, a solicitor cannot take action to recover it unless he first tells his client of the right, for the client, to require the bill to be referred to the Law Society for a 'remuneration certificate' or to have the bill 'taxed'. A remuneration certificate is a certificate stating whether, in the view of the Society, the charge made is fair and reasonable.

The Society is independently minded and will give a genuine and unbiased view. If it thinks the charge is too low, it says that the charge is reasonable and the solicitor cannot increase the account. If it thinks the charge is too high, it says so and certifies what it considers is a proper sum and the solicitor has to accept that. The client is on a 'heads I win, tails you lose' bet. He must, though, move quickly. He has only one month from the date of delivery of the bill to ask for the matter to be referred to the Law Society. Notice that only the client has the right to have the bill referred. The solicitor cannot go on his own accord.

If the Law Society says that the charge is reasonable, the client is even then still free to challenge the bill. He has another right; he can ask for the bill to be referred to the court for what is called 'taxation'. This means that an officer of the court goes through the bill, item by item, and the solicitor has to justify what he is charging. It is possible for the bill to be increased and if it is, the client must pay the sum found due. More than that, it is possible, if the bill is not reduced, for the client to be ordered to pay the costs of the taxation. So, if a client is not satisfied with the charge, the easiest and least dangerous course to take (from the client's point of view) is to ask for a remuneration certificate. Letter 13.8 is a letter to a solicitor asking him to obtain a remuneration certificate.

13.8

To a solicitor asking for the Law Society's remuneration certificate

Dear

On Thursday of last week I received your account for the work you undertook in connection with my recent acquisition of the shares in Brass Candlesticks Limited. I consider that the proposed amount is far in excess of the amount which is reasonable.

I remind you of your letter of 1 May 1988 in which you set out your basis of charging and quoted an hourly charging rate of £100. I cannot believe that you have spent 1,000 hours in the matter.

In the circumstances, I require you to refer your file to the Law Society and request that they issue a remuneration certificate in respect of your charges.

Yours sincerely

LETTER APPOINTING AN ACCOUNTANT AS AUDITOR

Every limited company must have its accounts audited. On the first meeting of the directors one of the tasks to be performed is appointment of an auditor. Quite apart from the demands of courtesy, before naming the auditor one should write to the chosen firm to ask if they will accept the appointment.

At the present time only members of the Institute of Chartered Accountants (of either England and Wales, Scotland or Ireland) or the Chartered Association of Certified Accountants are eligible for appointment. As with a solicitor, it is a wise precaution to check the fee that is likely to be charged. That will mean that the accountant will need to know what amount of work he has to do. It would be normal to expect him to agree the audited accounts with the Inland Revenue, but he will expect to charge extra if as well as auditing he is going to have to write up the books first.

Write Letter 13.9 and following his reply, if you are satisfied, appoint him at the appropriate meeting. Notice the request for advice on accounting year. If nothing is said and no 'notice of accounting reference date' is filed at the Companies Registry, the company's year will be to 31 March.

13.9

Appointing an auditor

Dear

This company has been newly incorporated and we are considering the appointment of auditor. Mr O. Jessup, manager of the Market Harborough branch of the Newbury Bank, has recommended that we approach your firm to enquire whether you would be willing to accept the appointment.

We shall be employing a full-time experienced bookkeeper and the accounts will be kept on an IBM personal computer using a standard bookkeeping package. We would ask our auditor to undertake the audit and subsequently settle the taxation problems that may arise.

Could you please indicate the fee that you would expect to charge for the service (assuming that you are willing to undertake it) and could you please recommend to us the accounting period we should adopt. Would you recommend 31 December year end, or 31 March, or perhaps some other date?

I await hearing from you with interest.

Yours sincerely

LETTER TO ACCOUNTANT ON ACQUISITION OF A BUSINESS

When a business is being purchased the help of an accountant is essential. This is especially true when what is being acquired is the shares in a limited company. The change of share ownership is irrelevant to the Inland Revenue, Commissioners of Customs and Excise and all creditors of the company. The company is responsible for its debts; the shareholders, whoever they are, will have to face the consequences. An accountant will investigate the financial affairs, will check the tax history (so far as he can) and will do what he can to see that the risks are minimised.

If he is in doubt or cannot get adequate answers to his questions he will let the solicitor acting know about it, so that property indemnities and warranties can be written into the purchase contract and, where appropriate, a reservation can be made from the purchase money to protect against future claims. Letter 13.10 is a letter of instruction to the accountant. The important points to cover are the basic terms of the deal that has been done, the name of the accountant acting for the seller, the name of the solicitor who is going to act, any particular matter that is concerning you and, finally, the prospective completion date.

13.10

Instructing accountant to investigate accounts on a purchase

Dear

We have been negotiating for the purchase of the entire issued share capital in the company Brass Candlesticks Limited. We have now agreed, subject to contract and to accountant's investigation, that we will pay £100 per share for each of the 1,000 ordinary shares in issue, and £50 per share for the 5,000 preference shares.

Can you please accept this letter as instructions to carry out a full investigation of the accounts and financial affairs of Brass Candlesticks Limited. Their accountants are Messrs Hunter, Jenner & Gray, and they have supplied us with the copies of the last three years' accounts which I now enclose.

We intend to instruct Messrs Peace, Haigh & Ellis as our solicitors and I am sending to Mr Peace of that firm a copy of this letter and asking him to liaise with you. I am suspicious that there may be undisclosed claims for previous tax years and possible creditors' claims which are outstanding. Will you in your investigation endeavour to check on this aspect and if, as may well be likely, you cannot obtain satisfactory replies, advise me and Mr Peace of your recommended retention that should be asked for on completion.

It is our wish that we work towards a completion date of 30 September next. Mr Cooper, the major shareholder in the company, has his sixty-fifth birthday on 31 August and we want to complete as soon as possible thereafter.

Yours sincerely

LETTER TO ACCOUNTANT INSTRUCTING TO APPEAL A TAX DEMAND

It is usual for the company auditor to agree with the revenue the tax liability of the company. In a small family company he also usually looks after the tax affairs of the principal shareholder. The revenue, particularly if accounts have not been filed and returns made, will often make an assessment based upon an estimate that is high enough to provoke response from the company. The first thing that is received is a notice of assessment. If this is ignored a notice to pay will follow. As soon as the notice of assessment is received send it to the accountant with Letter 13.11. The answer to the question raised about interest will almost certainly be 'pay the tax' because the taxation interest cannot, itself, be deducted whilst bank interest can. Still, it is nice to have the answer.

13.11

To accountant to appeal assessment

Dear

I enclose notice of assessment which I received this morning.

Will you please give the appropriate notice of appeal against this assessment and let me know whether you consider that any payment should be made on account of the liability that may ultimately be found due. I am, as you know, running this business on overdraft and would like to know whether the interest payable to the revenue on overdue tax would be more or less than the interest I will have to pay to the bank on the money I would be borrowing to pay the assessed tax.

Yours sincerely

LETTER TO ACCOUNTANT ASKING HIM TO PROVIDE A REGISTERED OFFICE

Every company has to register at the Companies Registry an address which is the place at which all official documents can be served. Writs, demands, formal notices of all kinds will be deemed properly served if they are sent to the registered office. It is usual to choose either the solicitor's or the accountant's office for this purpose. There is an advantage in choosing the accountant. The company's tax affairs are handled by the Inspector of Taxes for the district where the registered office is situated. If the accountant is handling the tax questions he will be known to, and he will know, the local inspector. Things move more smoothly when people know each other. It may help to ease difficulties if the inspector concerned is the accountant's local man. It may be that a charge will be made for providing the facility of the address. Write Letter 13.12 and then resolve on the registered office.

13.12

Asking permission to use the accountant's office as the registered office

Dear

Now that you have accepted appointment as our auditor, I wonder whether you would allow us to use your address as our registered office. If you would, will there be a charge and if so how much?

I hope that you can allow this. If you will let me know I will file the appropriate notice at the Companies Registry.

Yours sincerely

14

INSURANCE

REQUESTING COVER FOR A RISK

If it is wise to tell your solicitor, bank manager and accountant everything, it is doubly wise to be open with your insurers. Lawyers talk of insurance contracts as being contracts 'uberrimae fidei'. This means that there must be the utmost good faith shown by the insured, otherwise the insurance company can refuse to meet a claim (see Appendix 1). When requesting cover for any risk, make sure that the insurance company knows everything that is likely to be important. Letter 14.1 is a letter requesting cover for the company's business premises.

14.1

To an insurance company requesting cover

Dear Sirs

We enclose herewith completed proposal form for cover in the 'All Risks' policy that your company offers.

We think it right that we should elaborate on the replies to question 4. In question 4 you ask whether we have ever suffered any flooding and we have answered that we have not. This answer is correct but you should know that fifteen years ago, before we had any interest in this property, the Great Ouse river which runs on the opposite side of the road did overflow its banks as they were then and caused flooding here. Since that time the local water authority has carried out substantial works of culverting and installed flood prevention barriers upstream.

We await hearing from you with a quotation.

Yours faithfully

NOTIFICATION TO INSURERS

When anything happens that affects the cover or may give rise to a claim, the insurers should be notified. If a new piece of equipment is acquired which is going to be covered, notify insurers. Letter 14.2 notifies insurers of an increase in equipment. A description of the equipment and its value must be given. The insurance company may well ask for some proof of the value, particularly if the article in question is second-hand or was not acquired at arm's length. It is best to get this question of value settled at the time the cover is placed. If it is left until a claim arises the difficulty of proving value will be greater.

14.2

Notifying insurers of addition to equipment

Dear Sirs

You are holding cover under your 'All Risks' policy the office equipment used by us in this business.

We have purchased an IBM personal computer, value £1,500, and software consisting of a wordprocessing package, accounts package, databank package and spreadsheet, value £750. We wish these items to be added to the cover.

Please confirm that you agree the values, accept the risk and let us have a note of any increase in the premium payable.

Yours faithfully

MAKING A CLAIM

The insurance company will probably require claims to be made on their form. They should none the less be informed in detail and by letter of the claim. Letter 14.3 is an example. All details available of the loss should be indicated but make clear that at the moment a final statement of loss is not being made. It will often be found that only after a day or two is it noticed that some piece of property is not there. Get in all estimates for damage suffered before you close the claim.

14.3

Making a claim under an insurance policy

Dear Sirs

'All Risks' policy no. 12345

We regret to have to inform you that last night during the period when these premises were unoccupied, we suffered a break-in and thieves stole the equipment listed on the enclosed schedule. We are having further checks made to see whether any other property is missing.

In addition, they caused considerable damage to the property breaking down interior doors which were locked and forcing open the drawers of locked desks. Estimates are being obtained for the cost of carrying out the necessary repairs and these estimates, when obtained, will be sent to you for your acceptance.

The police have been informed and are making their enquiries. Meantime, would you please note that a claim will be made for the loss of the stolen goods, the damage to the property and the consequential loss caused to our business. Full details of these losses are being calculated and will be notified to you in due course.

Yours faithfully

PRODUCT LIABILITY AND PROFESSIONAL NEGLIGENCE COVER

If this is the age of the consumer, it is also the age of the litigator. Fortunately, in the United Kingdom we have not reached the position of the United States where lawyers take actions on the basis that they will receive a percentage of the winnings. Neither do we suffer the extravagantly high awards of damages which are common over there. None the less a defective product can mean a ruinous claim, apart from the even more ruinous bad publicity that results from a claim.

A solution is insurance. Product liability insurance and negligence cover is a specialised field in which few insurance companies will quote. It is best to employ a good broker and ask him to negotiate cover for you. He must be fully briefed on the product. Letter 14.4 is a letter to the broker instructing him. The information that will be needed is the value of the turnover, the nature of the product, the market in which sales are made and whether there is any sale of the product in the United States. They should also be told what, if any, claims have been received in the past.

NOTIFYING A THREATENED CLAIM

As soon as it seems possible that a claim may be made upon the business, if there is insurance cover, notify the insurance company and thereafter do not, in any circumstances, make any admission (do not even give some apology that could be construed as an admission) without the approval of the insurers. If you do, you may well find that the insurance company refuses to meet the claim. At the beginning of Chapter 5 (page 98) the point is made. It is repeated here because of its importance.

14.4

Instructing an insurance broker to obtain product liability cover

Dear Sir

Could you please obtain for us quotations for cover against claims which may arise from the sale of a defective product.

We manufacture candlesticks which are designed to be powered from the mains electricity. The materials from which the product is manufactured is an alloy which has the appearance of brass. It is non-conductive of electricity and is fully insulated.

All sales are made to the wholesale trade, no sales are made to consumers. We have a proportion (approximately 25 per cent of our output) which is sold to the United States of America. The total turnover this year is anticipated to be £2 million, which we hope will rise next year by at least 20 per cent. We require cover to protect us against all potential claims which arise out of the sales of the product and are alleged to be due to any defect in workmanship or materials. We have been in business for the past five years and at no time during that period have we had any claim or threat of a claim.

Yours faithfully

15

THE LEGAL IMPLICATIONS OF LETTERS

LIBEL

English law has grown from many different seeds. Unlike the majority of the laws in continental Europe, very little of our law is written down. 'Common Law', as we call it, is a fundamental law which is enforced in what used to be called the common law courts. It was the recognition by those courts of the principles, customs and rules of conduct which people used to observe.

The law of defamation has grown up in this way. When something is said about a person which would tend to make others think badly of him, that is a defamation. If it is in a permanent form, such as a letter, it is a libel. If it is spoken, it is a slander. In early days libel was a matter for the Church. It was punished with an award of damages, even though no loss could be shown. Slander was a matter for the common law courts which (except where the slander suggested a criminal act) would only give damages on proof of loss. So when writing a letter, thought must be given to what is being said lest someone can say they have been libelled. To constitute a libel needs three things. A wrongful statement that would tend to disparage someone; 'publication' of that statement to some third party (publication means intentionally communicating the information); and, lastly, the absence of any form of privileged occasion.

When you are asked to give a reference for an ex-employee, there is an obligation on you as described in Chapter 8. That obligation creates a privilege that entitles you to say what you really think, even though it may be defamatory of the ex-employee. The privilege can, though, be lost if you say what you say maliciously. That means that you are saying something with an improper motive: if, for example, you were deliberately trying to cause injury and prevent his being employed. In other cases the privilege is less likely to occur. Being a libel, anyone so defamed can bring an action without having to prove the damage he has

suffered. What is more, if the court thinks that the libel was a particularly grave matter, it can award exemplary damages. That means large
sums.

COPYRIGHT

When someone has created some work, a piece of writing, a painting, a
tune, some fruit of his brain, he is entitled to claim that it is his and to
make anyone who uses it pay for the privilege. The letters set out in this
book, for example, are in origin the subject of a claim for copyright. The
right to reproduce the work may be implied from the way in which the
work has been made available; these letters, or the precedent books in a
lawyer's office, have been made available and individually (not as a
collection) can be freely used without acknowledgement of their
authorship. Not everything is like that. If you write a letter (Letters 10.4
and 10.5, for example) and enclose with it a copy of a plan, the copyright
in the plan belongs to the architect who drew it, and he could object and
insist that he be paid for the use of his plan.

If you write to someone with a map showing the way to your office, if
the map was a copy of an ordnance survey sheet, you need a licence
from the Ordnance Survey Department for the reproduction. Any
quotation from a copyright work should acknowledge the source of the
work and only be made with permission of the author. These principles
apply just as much to the words of a letter as they do to a book. The
difference is that a letter has such a limited number of readers, and the
author has no thought of personal gain, so that any possibility of claim
being made can, in practice, be ignored.

USE IN LITIGATION

In Chapter 16 a brief description is given of the course of a matter that is
litigated. The most important part of the conduct of any proceedings is
the process which lawyers call 'discovery'. This is a process which is part
of all court proceedings in those parts of the world which use the
common law system. Basically that means the whole of what used to be
the British Empire and it includes the United States of America. Some
(especially the United States) have wider ranging powers of discovery
than we do here. All insist that all documents, including letters, which
have any relevance to the case must be disclosed. You must say, not
merely those that you have, but also those which have at any time been
in your 'possession or power'. You can be made to swear on oath to the
completeness of the list that you make.

Any letter that is written which may be read out in court must be very carefully thought about. It will be read in context and out of context. The language used will be considered critically and if it bears more than one possible meaning, the meaning most unfavourable to you will be chosen. That is why, time and again in this book, you are cautioned against trying to 'do it yourself'.

16

LITIGATION

THE CHOICE OF COURT

For the purposes of this work we will consider only High Court and County Court. In principle any action can be commenced in the High Court, but if the amount involved is less than £5,000 it is probable that at some stage in the proceedings it will be transferred to the County Court. The difference in procedure will be explained, but in general terms County Court proceedings are conducted with less complications and the costs are lower. If the dispute is one involving land or is seeking some special order, for example an order to restrain an ex-employee from competing, the action will almost certainly be better brought in the High Court.

COMMENCEMENT

In both courts the action starts by the plaintiff (the person who starts the proceedings) setting out in numbered paragraphs what his claim is. In the County Court this is referred to as the 'particulars of claim', whilst in the High Court it is called a 'statement of claim'. The claim sets out the basic facts which the plaintiff says he will prove which entitle him to whatever it is he asks the court to order. That claim must be brought within the time limits that the law has fixed for the various types of problem. As a generality, six years is the time for bringing an action to recover damages for a breach of contract or for things like negligence (as lawyers would say 'torts' – see Appendix 1). Once issued the proceedings have to be served upon the defendant.

In the County Court the court serves the claim by post. In the High Court it is up to the plaintiff to serve the claim. In the County Court the action starts with a summons to which the particulars of claim are attached. In the High Court the action starts with a writ which can either have the statement of claim typed on the back or go with it as a separate document. In the High Court the plaintiff has one year in which to serve the writ.

Now that is a thing to watch out for if you are the defendant. The time to bring proceedings may be six years. Six years may go by and no writ has been served. You are still not clear. The writ may have been issued but not served. Three hundred and sixty-four days later, you will be served and the plaintiff is still in time. Three hundred and sixty-six days later, if he has not served the writ, he is too late! (All right, 367 days if it is a leap year.) Having been served with a writ the defendant has fourteen days (including the day of service) to return to the court the form of acknowledgement of service that will come with the writ. In the County Court he has the same time in which to reply to the summons on the form that comes with it, saying whether or not the claim is contested.

This time limit is most important. If you are too late you may well find that the plaintiff has been to the court and obtained a judgment against you. Whenever you receive any document from the court or a writ, run straight to your solicitor. Time is against you.

DEFENCE

Having been served with the proceedings a defence has to be made. In the County Court, all of the documents, the particulars of claim, the defence, and the other things we shall mention, have to be filed in the court offices and go on the file that will eventually end up before the judge. In the High Court it is different. The writ is filed but thereafter all documents are sent to the solicitors for the parties, who keep them until the time comes to set the case down to be tried. The defence has to take each paragraph of the statement of claim (from here on we will concentrate on High Court) and give the defendant's answer to the point made. He may say, 'Yes, I admit that'; he may say, 'That is just not true'; he may say, 'That is true but because of this fact there is a different conclusion to be drawn.' He may simply say, 'No admission is made.' That means it is up to the plaintiff to prove it, if he can. What the defendant cannot do is simply say, 'I deny everything.' He has to take item by item and say whether or not he accepts it.

COUNTER CLAIM

The defendant may, in effect, want to say, 'All right, so I do owe you for this, but you owe me for that and what you owe me is more than I owe you.' He achieves this by making a counter claim. The defence will set out the answers to the statement of claim as indicated above. Probably that is an occasion when many of the answers will be, 'No admission is made', leaving the plaintiff to try to prove his case. Then the last paragraph of the defence will raise the 'set off' as a defence (a very technical matter – see Appendix 1).

The counter claim is just like a claim. It is included on the same sheet of paper as the defence and, indeed, the paragraph numbers continue on from the defence. It sets out, just like the claim, in numbered paragraphs what it is that the defendant says entitles him to some order of the court. To this counter claim, the plaintiff must deliver a defence.

SUMMARY JUDGMENT

A plaintiff can obtain a judgment without a full trial in two ways. First, if the defendant does not reply to the summons (in the County Court) or return the acknowledgement of service (in the High Court) within the fourteen days allowed. Secondly, in the High Court, the plaintiff can swear an affidavit saying that he believes there is no defence to his claim and then issue a summons (that is a way of bringing matters to the attention of the court and has to be served on the other party) to ask the court to give judgment accordingly. Served with such a summons, the defendant has to move quickly. He has to swear an affidavit which shows that he has got a defence. The dispute will not be decided there and then. It comes before a master of the High Court.

The master is a sort of minor judge. He reads both affidavits and he assumes, just for the sake of the argument, that what the defendant says is true. On the basis that it is true he decides whether that would amount to a defence. If he thinks it would, he lets the case go on. If he thinks that it does not show a good defence he will give judgment for the plaintiff. He can, if he wishes to, allow the case to go on the condition that the defendant pays into court the amount in dispute. This is the sort of order that would be made where the master had in his mind the thought that the defendant was merely playing for time.

Where the plaintiff is a foreigner or foreign company without any premises in the United Kingdom, or where there are reasonable doubts as to the solvency of the plaintiff, the master can order that the case be stopped until the plaintiff has given some security for the costs that the defendant will incur in defending the case.

JOINING THIRD PARTIES

The defendant may wish to say that what the plaintiff claims may well be true but someone else is really responsible for the trouble and should indemnify him against the consequences. For example, in the case suggested in Letter 7.5 where an agent wants to say that the responsibility is not his but the principal's; in that case he can issue what is called a 'third party notice'. That is very like starting proceedings between the defendant and the third party, and bringing the plaintiff, defendant and third party all together in the one case.

CLARIFYING THE ISSUES

The whole objective of this stage of the proceedings is to see that the question that the court has to decide is clearly defined. For this reason either party may require the other to give more details of his claims or allegations. Requests pass back and forth between them for 'further and better particulars'. If either of them does not want to give these particulars and argument starts whether or not they should, then back it goes to the master for him to adjudicate. Each of these stages is given a time limit. If more time is needed and the other side will not co-operate, back it goes to the master for him to adjudicate. If one of the parties is dragging his heels the other can go back to the master for him to order action or risk being struck out, that means 'you lose'. Eventually the issues are settled and we move to the next stage.

DISCOVERY

It is at this stage that the action can really be won or lost, and it is here that the importance of the various letters that have been written will become apparent. Both sides have to set out a list, in three parts, saying what documents they know about that bear on the case. Part one lists those documents which are in possession; part two lists those documents that were at some time or other in possession but are no longer. It must say what became of these missing documents. For example, a letter is written and as would be normal a carbon copy is kept. In part one you would say that you had the carbon copy whilst in part two you would say that once upon a time you had the original but you sent it to the addressee.

It is part three that can cause problems. There you say that you have certain documents but for some reason (which you have to explain) they are privileged and do not have to be disclosed. An obvious point of privilege is the correspondence you have with your solicitor. That is, in normal circumstances, privileged. Letters written 'without prejudice' may be privileged but, on the other hand, the privilege may have been lost or it may be that the 'without prejudice' description was not truly applicable. (See Chapter 5.) If there is any doubt, back we go to the master. It may be that there is a disbelief that all disclosure has been made; in that event the list may have to be supported on oath.

When lists have been made and exchanged, both sides inspect the documents that have been disclosed (except those that are privileged) and we are ready to go back to the master for directions as to the next step. There may be cases where some fact or other is peculiarly in the knowledge of the other party. The master can be asked to order him to answer on oath questions which will help to make clear just what the position is. The whole objective being to see that not only are the issues clear to the court, but also that neither side is unfairly being taken by surprise.

SETTING DOWN FOR TRIAL

Now the case is clear, both sides have made full disclosure of relevant documents and facts (but not the witnesses' names or any evidence by which those facts are to be proved) and the case is ready for trial. Back to the master and get an order to set down for trial. He will want to know how long it is anticipated the case will last and he will order the plaintiff to set down the case for hearing. Now, for the first time, the statement of claim, defence and the other particulars and documents that have been exchanged detailing the issues between the warring parties is delivered to the court, all neatly sewn up in two bundles.

The case is entered in the court list for trial. It may have been given a set day for the hearing. At present, time to ask for a fixed day would be usual, but because there are so many cases waiting trial this can be months or even years away. Alternatively it may be left to be called when the court can find a free slot. This may be quite quick. Cases fixed for trial on a fixed day may be settled or not take as long as anticipated. This leaves a judge free to take a case from the general list. That, though, means that you may get no more than twenty-four hours' warning that you are to be heard. Your barrister has organised his life to be in another court on that day, you have already decided that you were going away on holiday or have some vitally important meeting fixed with great difficulty for that day. You cannot help it. You must accept that another

barrister will have to take the case at very short notice and you will have
to abandon your meeting. It is because of these problems that a fixed day
is strongly favoured.

THE TRIAL

Now comes the trial. It is very unlikely that there will be a jury. There are
very few cases where you will hear the court drama so beloved of
playwrights; mostly they are dull unemotional debates between oppos-
ing barristers. They start by the barrister for the plaintiff outlining the
case and reading aloud the 'pleadings' (this is what the bundle of
statement of claim, defence, etc., is called) and the correspondence.

The two solicitors have agreed together which correspondence or
documents are going to be needed and they have prepared a bundle of
these for the court and everyone else. The plaintiff's barrister will then
refer to any particular legal point that arises and will read aloud the Acts
of Parliament and the decided cases that he is referring to. Having set the
scene, he will call the witnesses, who are examined, cross-examined
and re-examined.

Then it is the turn of the defendant. When the defence case has been
heard the barrister for the plaintiff addresses the judge and makes his
argument as to his case. The barrister for the defence answers him and
finally the judge gives his decision in a lengthy summary of the facts as
he has decided them to be and the law that follows from those facts.
Then follows argument as to who is to pay for all this.

The whole procedure takes many hours from the original issue of a
writ to the final judgment being delivered by the judge. Then comes the
problem of enforcing the judgment. But that is another story which can
take up nearly as much time and expense.

APPENDIX 1
GLOSSARY OF LEGAL WORDS AND EXPRESSIONS

Acceptance Every offer has to be accepted to create a contract. Acceptance can be in whatever form the person making the offer chooses. It can be by words or by conduct. The terms of the offer or the circumstances in which it is made may mean that there is no need to tell the person making the offer that it is accepted.

Appropriation The act of allocating to a contract the specific goods that are to be transferred. Once goods are taken from bulk and set aside, or once specific goods have been manufactured and set apart without any reservation or qualification to meet a particular order, they are appropriated to that order and the property (see below) in them passes to the purchaser.

Common law The inherent law that was applied in common to the whole of England. It was a recognition by the judges of the principles, rules and customs that existed. It became an expression to be used to distinguish between those rules and the rules of equity, and from there it has become extended to distinguish between the unwritten laws and the Acts passed by Parliament.

Consideration Some right, interest, profit or benefit given, or some forebearance, detriment, loss or responsibility given, suffered, or undertaken. Every contract must either be supported by consideration or be made under seal (see below). Without consideration the contract cannot be enforced. A contract under seal without consideration will be a good contract and will pass title to property from one person to another, but generally it cannot be specifically enforced. The 'consideration' must be given by the person who has received the offer. It must relate to some present or future action. Past actions, referred to as 'past consideration' will not be good enough to support a contract. So, an IOU given for an old debt has no consideration unless it is given, for example, 'in consideration of not commencing proceedings today'. Consideration does not have to be valuable, but it must be 'good'. Good consideration is consideration of blood relationship or of natural love and affection. So, 'in consideration of the natural love and affection of husband for wife' is good consideration (love of a man for his mistress is not considered in the same regard!), as is the consideration of the tie of blood between a man and his child. The consideration must not be illegal, any illegality makes the consideration void. Where the consideration offered does not materialise, it is said to have failed. Any money paid under a contract in which the consideration has wholly failed may be recovered.

Consumer   Neither the Consumer Credit Act 1974 nor the Sale of Goods (Implied Terms) Act 1973 gives any definition of the word 'consumer'. For the purposes of implied terms in a sale of goods (but not for credit sales), the word is generally taken to mean 'a *private* buyer from a *commercial* seller'.

Debenture   A form of mortgage given by a company. It may be specifically charged upon property or it may be left 'floating' which means that until some action is taken by the holder of the debenture, or some act that has been specified in the document takes place, no specific property is charged. When the act occurs or the debenture holder takes action, the floating charge is said to 'crystallise', which means that all the property of the company, its premises, its plant and machinery, even its book debts, become subject to the charge and can be taken by the debenture holder to satisfy his debt. The debenture may be one document, a series of documents or take the form of debenture stock, which can be bought and sold like any stocks or shares. The debenture holder has the usual rights of a mortgagee when his debt is due for repayment or when there is some default by the company. Most usually he will exercise his right to appoint a receiver to take charge of the company so as to sell the assets of the company to repay the debenture and any outstanding interest.

Equity   The common law (see above) did not provide all the remedies that were needed to do justice among the King's subjects. In some cases the rights given were too harsh. The Lord Chancellor, who was always a clergyman, was considered to be the keeper of the King's conscience and in that capacity he would come forward with a remedy to give an equitable solution to a problem. Courts under the control of the Lord Chancellor were established to deal with these cases and those special Courts of Equity existed right up to the 1870s, when the modern High Court was established. The rules of equity are still applied, and problems involving an equitable remedy are usually (but not exclusively) tried in the Chancery Division. The most common equitable remedies to be met by business men are injunctions and specific performance.

Frustration   Something unforeseen that has prevented a contract being performed because the subject matter or the basic principles upon which the bargain was struck have been destroyed or no longer exist. It is a question of construction of the terms of the contract to decide whether the act that has occurred goes to the heart of the contract and frustrates it. Any money paid under a frustrated contract can be recovered.

Injunction   An injunction is one of the equitable remedies. It can take two forms: restrictive, or mandatory. At common law, if a man was injured by the wrongful action of another, all he could ask for was damages. This might not be a good enough remedy and the Courts of Equity came forward to give relief by ordering the wrongdoer to stop doing whatever it was that was wrong (a restrictive injunction) or to do something that he ought to do (a mandatory injunction). The common law courts always enforced their orders against a man's property, so damages meant that goods might be taken in satisfaction. Equity acted differently. Equitable remedies were directed against the individual, and if he did not obey he was imprisoned. So, today, breach of an injunction is enforced by an application to commit to prison, whilst non-payment of damages is enforced by sale of assets.

Innuendo   Innuendo is the meaning that is implied by words or actions that otherwise sound or look innocent. For example, in one case a waxwork of a man was exhibited. That seemed innocent enough. But it was exhibited together with the models of three others all of whom were criminals. The innuendo being that the man was a criminal. Whenever it is alleged that words which, on the face of them are perfectly innocent, bear an innuendo, the innuendo must be explained.

Lien   Although the word has a wider meaning, the most usual meaning given by lawyers to a lien is what is technically called a possessory lien. This is the right for a person to retain the goods of another as security for a debt due to him. The lien arises either by the legal right that is given to certain classes of creditors, or by the agreement between the parties which created the debt. The principal liens arising by law are, for payment to a workman for his work on the goods upon which he has done the work, for a solicitor for his fees on the papers and documents of the client, for a banker for moneys due to him on property of his customer and for an innkeeper on the goods of his guest for the charges due. It is open to anyone making a contract to ask for a lien. Carriers frequently ask for a lien on the goods being carried.

Liquidator The man appointed either by the court, by the shareholders or by the creditors of a company which is to be wound up. Following the passing of the Insolvency Act 1976 only authorised insolvency practitioners (usually chartered accountants but some solicitors have also been approved) can be appointed. Once the company goes into liquidation all the directors are automatically removed from office and the liquidator exercises their powers. In a winding up by the court it is usual for the official receiver to be appointed liquidator in the first place. Later, the creditors can replace him by a liquidator of their choice. The liquidator differs from a receiver (see below) in that the liquidator is only appointed where the company is in liquidation and he acts in the place of the directors, realising all the assets of the company for the benefit of the creditors of the company. The receiver is acting solely for the benefit of the creditor who has appointed him. The appointment of a liquidator does not take priority over a receiver who has been appointed and has taken possession of the company's assets.

Mitigation It is the duty of anyone who has been injured either from some tort (see below) or breach of contract to minimise the losses he will suffer. This is called mitigation.

Moratorium An agreement that a debt which is lawfully and currently due may remain unpaid for the time being.

Novation The replacement of one party to a contract with someone else. When two people make a contract, they may agree that the benefit of the contract can be assigned. Assignment of the contract, though, will not release either of them from their obligations. A lease, for example, is a contract. When it is assigned, the original tenant still remains liable on the lease, and if the assignee does not pay the rent, the landlord can claim on the original tenant. The only way in which the original tenant can escape liability is if the landlord will agree to a novation. That would entail a deed in which the landlord agrees to release the original tenant and accept the assignee in his place. The same principal applies to all contracts.

Property The right of ownership to real estate or goods. The right does not necessarily carry with it the right to possession, for example someone else may have a lien on goods or someone else may have a charge on them. Property exists in goods, rights such as patents, trade marks and copyright, debts and real estate. It can be transferred with or without possession.

Quantum meruit   Literally, 'as much as he has earned'. Where a price has not been agreed upon beforehand the court will award a just payment for the services that have been rendered. It will apply where no price was agreed or where a contract has not been fully performed due to the default of the other party. In that case the party not in default can claim 'quantum meruit' for the services he has performed.

Receiver   A man appointed either by a mortgagee or by the court as a means of recovery of a debt, to take over the running of a business or possession of a property, and receive the income or sell the assets or property, and apply the proceeds in discharge of the debt. Whilst he is in possession he acts as agent of the company. Unlike the case of a liquidator, the appointment of a receiver does not discharge the directors, but they are effectively impotent because he has all the rights to the property and assets of the company, and he alone can operate the business. He may be appointed simply 'receiver' or he may be appointed 'receiver and manager'. If he is only receiver he is only empowered to collect in the income and assets. If he is receiver and manager he may run the business as a going concern taking the profits for his creditor. The company will often be put into liquidation after the receiver has been appointed (because the other creditors are not being paid), but the liquidator must wait until the receiver has been discharged before he can take over, and then he takes whatever is left.

Representation   A statement or assertion made by one party to the other, before or at the time of the contract, of some matter or circumstance relating to it. If the representation was relied upon by the other party and it was false, the other party has the right to set the contract aside. It does not matter whether the false statement was made knowing that it was untrue or if it was quite an innocent error. The representation must, though, have been something upon which the other party relied and persuaded him to enter into the deal. (In lawyers' language, it was a representation inducing the contract.)

Repudiation   The act of refusing to perform the contract. A breach of one of the terms of the contract may be so serious that it shows that the party concerned does not consider himself bound by the contract and it will in that event amount to a repudiation. It will be for the other party to decide whether to accept this or not. (See Chapter 3, page 54).

Retention of title   The property in goods (see above) usually passes when the goods are delivered. It is possible for the seller of the goods to specify that this will not happen, but that he will retain the property and the right to repossess the goods if they are not paid for. A clause to this effect has to be included in the conditions of sale for the right to arise. Such a clause is commonly referred to as a retention of title clause. Lawyers may refer to it as a 'Romalpa' clause after the name of the case that was decided and upheld the legal principle on which the clause is based.

Seal Contracts can be executed (that means authenticated in some way), either 'under hand' or 'under seal'. In the first case a simple signature is all that is required. In the case of a limited company (which does not have a hand by which to sign anything) the signature has to be by someone who is duly authorised to sign for the company. Usually it is a director or the secretary. In the case of a contract 'under seal' there has to be not only a signature but also some form of seal. In earlier days, hot wax would be put on to the document and an impression of the individual's seal would be pressed into it. Today it is more usual to have a small round, red, plastic wafer stuck on to the document. The document then has to be 'signed' (signature is obvious), 'sealed' (that means sticking on the plastic wafer and placing a finger on to it), 'and delivered'. Delivery means bringing the deed into full and unconditional effect. It is possible to deliver a deed 'in escrow', which means that the delivery is made on a condition. In that case the condition of the escrow would have to be stated. The difference between a document under hand and one under seal is that the document under seal is effective even without the support of consideration (see above), also any action based upon the breach of the terms of a contract under hand must be brought within six years of the breach. In the case of a contract under seal the time is doubled to twelve years.

Set off A set off is a cross-claim by the defendant to a claim by the plaintiff. The amount to be set off will be equal to or less than the amount due from the defendant to the plaintiff. It takes the form of a defence to the claim. If a sum larger than that claimed by the plaintiff is claimed by the defendant, the defendant would make a counter claim for the amount he claims to be his due and claim to set off so much of that sum as is necessary to extinguish the plaintiff's claim. Claims of any kind, debt or damages can be set off against each other.

Specific performance An order of the court that a party to a contract carry out his contractual obligations. The order will only be made where damages for breach of contract would be an inadequate compensation. The most usual cases are in the sale of land where one party has failed to complete. No order for specific performance will be made unless valuable (as distinct from good) consideration has been given (see above).

Tort   A wrong independent of contract. It is the breach of a duty owed by one person to another (as in negligence where the duty is to take care), the interference with the rights of another (as in the case of a trespass) or in the breach of a duty imposed by law. Circumstances can (and often do) arise where the wrong is both a breach of contract and a tort. For example, negligence by a professional man can be a breach of contract, because the contract implies a term that the work will be properly done, and a tort, because a duty of care is owed to the client.

Uberrimae Fidei   Literally, the utmost good faith. Some contracts, insurance being the most common, require the parties to observe the utmost good faith to each other. The insured must disclose everything that bears upon the assessment of the risk. It is different from the ordinary contract for the sale of property where the rule is 'let the buyer beware' (*caveat emptor*) and there is no obligation on the vendor to disclose defects.

Warranty   A term of the contract which is collateral to the main purpose of the contract. In a sale of goods, the main purpose is to transfer ownership from one person to another. As a term of that sale there are implied by law certain warranties, for example, in a sale by sample that the bulk of the goods will correspond with the sample. That warranty is not the main purpose of the contract but it underlies it. Breach of the warranty will give rise to a claim for damages. This is in distinction to a condition of the contract where a breach will give the right to rescind the contract. It is a fine distinction and in each case it depends upon the construction of the contract whether the term in question is a warranty or a condition.

APPENDIX 2
CONDITIONS OF SALE

The following is a fairly standard set of conditions of sale. After each condition there is a note in brackets explaining the reason for the condition.

DEFINITIONS

In these conditions the following applies:

1. 'The Company' means Brass Candlesticks Ltd.
2. 'The Customer' means the person, company or corporation who has placed an order with the company.
3. 'The Goods' means the goods sold under these conditions of sale.

[In any formal document where words are going to be used in a special manner, a definition clause is essential. For example, 'The Company': in all probability both the seller and the buyer will be limited companies, therefore say which of them is going to be meant when the term is used. In the same way, use a capital letter to show that the word is being used in a special sense.]

GENERAL

1. These conditions shall govern any sale of goods by the Company to the exclusion of any other terms and conditions except such terms and conditions as have been expressly approved of in writing by a director of the Company.

[Obviously the whole point of having conditions of sale is to be able to know where you are when any difficulty arises, so make them apply to all sales. Some degree of flexibility is needed but do not allow any Tom, Dick or Harry to alter them. Keep control over the situation by confining authority to vary the conditions to a limited class of people.]

2. Any quotation given by the Company shall be construed as an invitation to treat and orders placed thereon are subject to acceptance by the Company.

[This is changing the ordinary understanding of a quotation as being an offer. It means that this is no more than an indication to a customer of the basis upon which his offer would be accepted. It means that when he sends in his order, that is the offer and the Company can accept it or not as it wishes. When his order comes in, remember the battle of the forms and check that his order does not contain contradictory terms.]

3. Unless otherwise expressly stated therein a quotation shall not remain open for more than twenty-eight days from the date of the quotation. A quotation may be withdrawn at any time.

[Although the quotation is not an offer, the principles explained in Chapter 2 (page 38) are equally applicable.]

PRICES

1. The Company reserves the right to increase prices (whether specifically quoted or not) to take account of increases in the cost of raw materials, wages, taxes, insurance, manufacture, packing, or transport arising before despatch.
2. Prices are exclusive of VAT or other tax, duty, tariff or charge, arising in the United Kingdom or elsewhere.
3. Unless otherwise agreed, prices are ex-works, carriage and packing extra.
4. If at the request of the Customer or by reason of any action or inaction of the Customer work on the contract or delivery of the goods is suspended, the Company shall have the right both to increase the purchase price and to alter the time of delivery.

[These provisions are self-explanatory. They are inserted purely for commercial reasons and have no especial legal significance.]

DELIVERY DATES

1. Any dates given for shipment or delivery are approximate.
2. Whilst every effort will be made to adhere to the agreed dates, such dates are not guaranteed and the Company accepts no liability for delay in shipment or delivery from any cause whatsoever.

[In a commercial contract, unless something is said, the law assumes that 'time is of the essence'. This means that any reference to time is a vital matter and failure to keep to the time gives a right to damages. These two clauses make it clear that in this case, time is not 'of the essence'.]

3. The Company may, at its discretion, deliver the goods in instalments.

[Without this clause there is no right to make part delivery, which can sometimes be inconvenient.]

4. The Company shall have a lien on all goods appropriated to this contract, the title to which have passed to the Customer, for all sums due from the Customer to the Company, whether arising under the contract of sale or not.

[See Chapter 6 (page 126) and Appendix 1 for definitions of 'lien'.]

5. Where the Customer, having been notified that the Goods are ready for despatch or, as the case may be, for collection, for any reason refuses or is unable to accept delivery or to make collection the Company shall be entitled to invoice the Customer for the agreed price of the Goods (which the Customer shall pay as though the Goods had been despatched or collected on the date of notification), the Company shall have the right to charge the Customer for storage and insurance of, and all other expenses incurred by it in respect of, the Goods and, notwithstanding the 'Passing of title and risk' clause below, risk in the Goods shall be treated as having passed to the Customer from the date of the Company's notification.

[This covers that unfortunate position where for one reason or another the Customer holds up delivery. Without this clause, the goods would effectively be warehoused free for the Customer. With the clause the Company can charge for storage. 'Passing of title and risk' (pages 349–51) is the retention of title clause. It is possible to say that although ownership has not passed the risk of damage or loss has. This is similar to the law in the case of a sale of a house where, from the date contracts are exchanged, the property is at the risk of the purchaser. This clause is applying the same principle to a sale of goods.]

WARRANTY AND LIABILITY

1. Subject to sub-clauses 2, 3, 4, 5 and 6 the Company warrants the Goods against the following:

(a) departure from its usual standards and specifications, or, in the case of goods manufactured to the Customer's specification, departure from the Customer's specification, and defects in materials and workmanship, which become apparent under normal use within twelve months of delivery of the Goods and which are notified to the Company within twenty-eight days of their becoming apparent;

[This clause makes clear that the Company will manufacture the goods according to the appropriate specification. If there are defects in workmanship or materials, or the Company does not manufacture the goods to the agreed specification, it is probable that even without this warranty, the Customer will have a claim. The express warranty does, though, give the Customer some comfort.]

(b) breach of industrial property rights of which the Company is aware at the date of the contract, except in respect of designs provided by the Customer.

[This is an assurance that the Company is not manufacturing in breach of some patent or similar right.]

2. If the Goods or any part of them do not comply with the foregoing clauses the Company will, at its reasonable option replace the same, rectify the breach, refund the appropriate part of the price or take back all or part of the Goods. Any goods replaced by the Company shall become the property of the Company and shall be held by the Customer to the order of the Company.

[This is an attempt to limit the damages that the Company would otherwise have to pay for its breach of contract.]

3 The Company shall not be liable for any of the following:
(a) design defects, unless new design work is necessary specifically to fulfil the contract;

[This is using the maxim 'let the buyer beware' and putting the onus on the Customer to satisfy himself that the design is suitable. Where the contract puts an obligation on the Company to design the product specially, the Company will be liable for bad design as 'bad work'.]

(b) consequential loss;

[Unless this was expressly excluded the breach of contract would give rise to damages for all damages that could reasonably have been foreseen.]

(c)   any excess in total claims over the contract price.

[This is limiting liability to the contract price. It is permissible to limit damages in this way except in the case of some liabilities in consumer sales. Where the parties are not of equal bargaining strength, clauses excluding liability have to be 'reasonable'.]

(d)   technical advice or assistance which it was not contractually bound to provide;

[There is always a risk in giving free help. Even though it is a generous act you can be liable in damages for anything which is considered negligent. This clause excludes that risk.]

(e)   loss caused by delay;

[This is another 'time not of the essence' clause.]

(f)   any loss which the Company is precluded from recovering from a carrier by reason of the Customer's failure to give the notice necessary for such recovery;

[Most contracts of carriage provide that where goods are damaged in transit notice has to be given at the time. Since only the Customer will have a chance to check this it seems fair that if he does not give notice the Company should be relieved of any responsibility.]

(g)   any alleged defect in the Goods which the Customer or any person acting on its behalf shall have rectified or attempted to rectify;

[This is self-explanatory.]

(h)   any failure or delay in the performance of its obligations caused by any circumstances beyond its reasonable control;

[Again, self-explanatory.]

(i)   damage caused by misuse or non-compliance with instructions set out in the Company's instructions (if any).

[Self-explanatory.]

4.   The Company does not exclude or limit liability for death or personal injury arising from negligence.

[This is expressly set out although under the Sale of Goods (Implied Terms) Act such liability cannot be excluded.]

5. In the case of goods supplied which have not been manufactured by the Company, the Company will (so far as possible) assign to the Customer the benefit of any warranty made by the manufacturer of the Goods or the person who supplied them to the Company or, subject to a suitable indemnity being given to it by the Customer for any costs or liabilities incurred or undertaken by the Company in respect thereof, will use its best endeavours to enforce such warranty for the benefit of the Customer.

[Warranties that the Company has received may be assignable, in which case they will be assigned to the Customer. The Customer must give a notice of the assignment to the company who gave the warranty to enable the Customer to sue on the assignment. Otherwise the Customer would have to sue in the name of the Company. Where the warranties are not assignable, then the only way they can be enforced for the Customer is by the Company taking action. It is only obliged to do this if it gets a suitable indemnity against the costs, etc., involved.]

6. The warranties given in these conditions are personal to the Customer and are not capable of being assigned.

[This means that only the Customer has the benefit of the warranties and he cannot enforce them for the benefit of someone else.]

7. The Company will deliver with the Goods a delivery note and unless the contents of the note are disputed by the Customer within seven working days after the date recorded upon it the particulars shown upon it shall be conclusive as against the Customer.

[This is designed to make the Customer raise any claims at once.]

8. Any description of goods appearing in the Company's advertising or in a catalogue or literature produced by the Company is given by way of identification only and the use of such a description shall not constitute a sale by description. In so far as information contained in such advertising catalogue and literature has been compiled from information supplied to the Company by any other party the Company accepts no responsibility for its accuracy.

[Certain implied warranties are given in the case of a sale by description. This clause makes clear that this is not a sale by description. The final sentence of the clause is an attempt to show that the advertising literature, etc., was not a representation upon which the Customer should rely.]

FORCE MAJEURE

The Company shall be excused non-delivery or delay in delivery directly or indirectly caused by or resulting from, or made fundamentally more onerous by, events or circumstances beyond the Company's reasonable control (including but without prejudice to the generality of the forego- ing, suppliers' delays and trade disputes, whether of the Company's employees or otherwise). In the event of any deliveries being so suspended or delayed, the period of the contract shall be correspond- ingly extended, or if deliveries are suspended for six months or more either party may, by notice in writing to the other, cancel the contract whereupon the Company shall either issue a credit note or invoice as appropriate, in an amount equal to an equitable portion of the total contract price.

[This is attempting to deal with the sort of problem that arises when a contract becomes frustrated as described in Chapter 3 (page 58). Here the underlying basis has gone because of some supervening event.]

PAYMENT

1. Payment shall be nett and without set off, so as to be received on or before the end of the month following the month of delivery of the Goods. The Company shall be entitled to charge simple interest on overdue accounts at a rate of 0.05 per cent per day.

[As explained in Chapter 4 (page 92), there is no right to charge interest on a delayed payment unless the contract provides for it. This is the way to provide for it.]

2. The time for performance of the Customer's obligations (whether as to payment or otherwise) shall be of the essence so that failure to perform in respect of one delivery shall entitle the Company at its option to cancel, or delay that delivery or other deliveries or to treat the whole contract as repudiated by the Customer.

[This makes time of the essence against the Customer. It is taking the point made in Chapter 3 (page 56) and providing that a breach of this provision is a fundamental breach.]

PASSING OF TITLE AND RISK

1. Notwithstanding that the Customer obtains possession of the Goods, both the legal and the equitable title thereto will remain in

the Company until the Company has received payment from the Customer of the contract price in full with all VAT thereon and all other moneys that may be or become due from the Customer to the Company in relation thereto. Until such time, the Customer shall hold the Goods in trust for the Company and the Company shall be entitled to require the Customer to deliver the Goods or any of them to it on demand and to enter upon the Customer's premises for the purpose of collecting them (to include, without prejudice to the generality of the foregoing, the dismantling of any item into which the Goods have been incorporated) and the Customer shall be responsible for all the Company's costs and expenses in connection with so doing. The Customer may, however, subject to clause 2 below, sell the Goods by way of bona fide sale in the ordinary course of its business on its standard terms and conditions and by way of sale as principal (not as agent). That sale will constitute a sale by the Customer of the Company's property and accordingly the Customer will account to the Company for the proceeds of sale up to the amount outstanding in respect of the Goods and pending such accounting will hold the same in trust for the Company.

[This is a form of retention of title clause making it clear that until payment of all money due to the Company the goods remain the Company's property. To reinforce its position the Company makes the Customer declare that it is a trustee for the Company and give the Company a right to go onto the Customer's premises to repossess the goods when it wants to. It is recognised that the Customer may have purchased the goods for resale and rather than create problems for the Customer's customers, the Company gives the Customer freedom to sell but any purchase money belongs to the Company up to the amount owing on the goods.]

2. The Customer's right given or implied from sub-clause (a) of this clause to retain possession of and deal with the Goods shall automatically and without notice be determined forthwith in any of the following circumstances:
   (a) if the Customer continues in breach of any of the terms hereof following the service upon the Customer of a notice in writing sent by or on behalf of the Company complaining of the breach;
   (b) if the Customer (being an individual) is adjudged bankrupt or suffers any execution to be levied upon any of his assets;
   (c) if the Customer (being a company) has a receiver appointed of

all or any part of its property or passes any resolution for creditors winding up or is unable to pay its debts within the meaning of section 518 of the Companies Act 1985 or is in arrear with any sum due from it hereunder.

[This clause is necessary to protect the Company from any claim by a creditor who is trying to execute a judgment or by any receiver or liquidator who wants to claim that the goods are available for them to take. The clause takes automatic effect and means that the Company can immediately repossess the goods or take the proceeds of sale of any of the goods that have been sold.]

3. On the occurrence of any of the events specified in clause 2 above, the Company may (without prejudice to any other rights or remedies available to it) without notice determine all or any part of this contract and may suspend or cancel deliveries hereunder and shall have a general lien on all the Customer's property then in the possession of the Company (whether as consignee or otherwise) in respect of any sums which may be owing by the Customer to the Company on any account whatsoever, and on the expiration of fourteen days' notice the Company shall be entitled to dispose of the same and apply the proceeds of the sale towards satisfaction of all moneys owing to the Company.

[This clause has two objectives: firstly, it puts an end to the contract and stops any receiver or liquidator claiming that the Company must fulfil the order; secondly, it gives the Company a full lien on any property of the Customer that is still in the Company's hands. For example, the Customer may have just paid up in full for one consignment which is still with the Company waiting delivery (so that that particular set of goods does belong to the Customer) and gives the Company a power of sale over the goods which are the subject of the lien.]

EXPORT DELIVERIES

In respect of all contracts for the sale of goods outside the United Kingdom the Customer will provide any necessary export licences, import licences or exchange control authorisations within a reasonable time prior to the date for shipment.

[Self-explanatory. Whilst much of the licensing for export and all exchange control has been removed so far as the UK authorities are concerned, other countries still impose restrictions that have to be complied with to permit shipment to their shores.]

RETURN OF PACKAGES

1. The Company will pack goods in accordance with its normal practice.
2. A charge may be made for all pallets drums packing cases or returnable packages. Full credit for the amount charged will be given if they are returned to the point of despatch carriage paid and in good and undamaged condition within three months of the date of the invoice.

[It has to be made clear whether the packing is or is not part of the sale. If the Customer wants special packaging he must order it. If the packaging is charged for on a returnable basis, this also must be made clear.]

ASSIGNABILITY

1. The Customer may not assign or part with its interest in this contract.

[A contract is normally assignable and the assignee, once he has given notice of the assignment to the other party to the contract takes all the benefits of the contract. In a large contract it may be that the personality of the Customer is very important. It is one thing to undertake a contract for a million pounds of business for a large public company but quite different to take the same risks and liabilities for a one-man band. Even though, without a novation, the original party would remain liable it is wise to retain control. The original party might be a limited company which after it had assigned the contract went into liquidation. This clause stops the Customer parting with his interest in the contract.

2. The Company may delegate or sub-contract its duties under this contract but shall despite such delegation or sub-contract remain liable to the Customer for the full performance thereof.

[The Customer is entitled to require the Company to carry out all the work itself unless the contract otherwise provides. This clause is giving the Company the right that it is denying to the Customer in the previous clause and provides for sub-contracting.]

INTERPRETATION

These conditions and the contract of which they form a part shall be governed by and construed in accordance with English law and the

Customer irrevocably submits to the jurisdiction of the English Courts.

[Particularly if there is any foreign element in the contract it is important to declare which law is to apply and the Courts which are to try disputes.]

INDEX